A Concise Introduction to Bernard Lonergan, S.J

John P. Cush, STD

En Route Books and Media, LLC

Saint Louis, MO

⊕ENROUTE
Make the time

En Route Books and Media, LLC
5705 Rhodes Avenue
St. Louis, MO 63109

Cover credit: Sebastian Mahfood

ISBN-13: 979-8-88870-401-1 and 979-8-88870-407-3
Library of Congress Control Number:
Available online at https://catalog.loc.gov

Dedicated to the memory of my mother,
Catherine Cush

Acknowledgments

I am very grateful to Brother Loyce Pinto, M.Id., for his careful reading of this text and for being a great dialogue partner, always seeking to clarify my own expression of Lonergan and Doran's thought. In addition, my gratitude must go to those professors who had introduced Lonergan to me: Msgr. Conrad Dietz, Msgr. Richard Liddy, and especially Fr. Gerard Kevin Whelan, S.J.

Table of Contents

Introduction

What is Theological Method? Why is it needed?

When describing one's primary theological interest as method, the reaction that one usually receives is one of incomprehension by those who are not familiar with theological studies. Why should a topic as personal as theology, which involves the study of God and the things of God have a particular methodology imposed on it? C. S. Lewis responds to this question concerning the absolute need to clarify terminology, to set limitations and to generally have a clear, concise, roadmap before engaging in any level of serious study. Lewis writes:

> The first qualification for judging any piece of workmanship from a corkscrew to a cathedral is to know what it is—what it was intended to do and how it is meant to be used. After that has been discovered the temperance reformer may decide that the corkscrew was made for a bad purpose, and the communist may think the same about the cathedral. But such questions come later. The first thing is to understand the object before you: as long as you think the corkscrew was meant for opening tins or the cathedral for entertaining tourists you can say nothing to the purpose about them.[1]

Therefore, in other words, one needs to understand the method before one can understand the theology. Likewise, one needs to

---

[1] C. S. Lewis, *A Preface to Paradise Lost* (Oxford: Oxford University Press, 1960), 1.

understand the theological method employed by a particular theologian before one can grasp the theology which he or she is mining from the fonts of revelation, namely Sacred Scripture and Sacred Tradition, as well as how he or she views the lived experience of culture as a source of theology. J. J. Mueller writes: "Because method never sits apart from the theologian who wields it or from the content of theology that is generated, the task is a challenging one."[2]

Difficult, too, is the attempt to explain not only the need for a theological method in general, but also its pastoral significance. For many in Christian ministry, very little conscious time is spent pondering [on] the issue of theological method, but it really is of the utmost importance in the Christian endeavor. Mueller states: "But whenever we ask ourselves how we arrived at an answer, then we are raising the method question. Method is done best by reflecting over how we actually arrived at an answer. Method then reflects upon reflecting."[3]

This "reflection upon reflecting" has important implications for the Church in her attempts at the evangelization of culture. What manner, what approach should one bring to the transmission of the Christian faith? Jared Wicks, concerning the essential nature of having a proper theological method, writes:

> The articulation of a coherent system, built up from insights into the theological sources, must also relate to the evangelizing and pastoral mission of the church. Contemporary

---

[2] J. J. Mueller, *What are they saying about Theological Method* (Ramsey, N.J.: Paulist Press, 1984), 2.

[3] Ibid., 1.

systematic theologies are evaluated according to their potential to enhance Christian proclamation in the great socio-cul-
tural religions of the world. Theologians read the sources and
elaborate their systems in particular cultural settings. Their
explanations must point toward forms of Christian life, wor-
ship, and teaching that correspond to their culture. Theology
stands in the service of this inculturation of our common
faith in God's offer of new life.[4]

Bernard J. F. Lonergan writes: "A theology mediates between a cultural matrix and the significance and role of a religion in that matrix."[5] Since this is apparent, as a normative, classicist notion of culture is left behind and attempt to speak of God and the things of God
in a world that often seems to have forgot God, a clear, concise
method is essential in a study of a theologian's life's work. "Method
is not a set of rules to be followed meticulously by a dolt. It is a framework for collaborative creativity."[6] Theological method is not an ex-
cessively academic, overly cerebral activity for only certain fundamental theologians. It is part and parcel of the entire theological enterprise and has ramifications for the pastoral activity of the Church.
Without a firm grounding in a proper theological method, even the
best attempts to evangelize the culture will fall flat. The woven cloth
of pastoral ministry will quickly become frayed and begin to unravel
at the seams without a clear theological method. Those who attempt

---

[4] Jared Wicks, *Introduction to Theological Method* (Casale Monferrato:
Piemme, 1994), 9.

[5] Bernard J. F. Lonergan, *Method in Theology* (New York: Seabury Press,
1972), xi.

[6] Ibid.

theology and those who attempt to engage in ministry without knowing theological method will be like the foolish builder in the parable in Matthew 7:26-27- "And every one then who hears these words of mine and does not do them will be like a foolish man who built his house upon the sand; and the rain fell, and the winds blew and beat against that house, and it fell; and great was the fall of it."[7] In my opinion, the master of theological method in the Catholic Anglophone world is Bernard Lonergan.

Why Lonergan?

For a certain generation of those who studied theology, namely those who came of age in their theological studies in the 1960s and 1970s, the name of Bernard J.F. Lonergan was constantly referenced. For my generation of theologians, when one mentions Lonergan, it is all too often looked at askance. For many, Lonergan is neither fish nor fowl. For some, he is not sufficiently radical enough, considered too indebted to Tradition. To others, his thought is considered not sufficiently Thomistic, far too eclectic in his thought. And still, there are others who point to him as the one providing the blueprint for the philosophy behind a relativistic theology of pluralism with his development of the concept of historical consciousness.

I have been asked if my interest in Lonergan is merely a historical curiosity, a desire to look into a period of time in Catholic theology that has since passed. To be honest, the more that I consider that

---

[7] All Sacred Scripture citations are taken from *The New Oxford Annotated Bible with the Apocrypha, Expanded Edition, An Ecumenical Study Bible, Revised Standard Version* (Oxford: Oxford University Press, 1977).

question, I must admit that this is partly true. After I had defended and published my doctorate in theology at Rome's Pontifical Gregorian University, which involved a study of John Courtney Murray through the lens of both Bernard Lonergan and Robert Doran, my doctoral director actually asked me if I was really as interested in theology as much as the history of theology. I am fascinated by the way that thought develops, especially in the Western theological tradition.

Further, I have been questioned, continually, in some circles, asked if Lonergan has really anything to offer in an all-too fractured theological world. The answer to the question of whether Lonergan has anything to offer for theology today is one to which I believe that I can confidently respond with an affirmative. In the history of 20th Century Roman Catholic theology, are there figures who have had and will no doubt have more influence in the "long run" that Bernard J.F. Lonergan? I believe that de Lubac, Congar, Balthasar, Chenu, Ratzinger, Rahner, and Garrigou-Lagrange, just to name a few, have had a greater impact on Roman Catholic theology *in toto* than Lonergan. I do not believe that this is a debatable issue. Lonergan himself did not help to draft any of the documents of the Second Vatican Council. One can examine the documents of the Second Vatican Council and attempt to ascertain where Lonergan's influence might have been present (one needs to look only to the work of John Courtney Murray, especially in the immediate time period leading up to the drafting of *Dignitatis Humanae*).

Lonergan's thought, at this time in the history of Catholic theology, is largely limited to Anglophones with only a few non-English speakers demonstrating a real interest in his thought. And yet, some of whom he has influenced, those who have used his theology, for better or for worse (and this is not the place for me to debate the use or the misuse of Lonergan's theological concepts, especially historical consciousness), have influenced thousands of students of theology over the years.

Bernard Lonergan is a key and vital figure in the history of 20th Century theology. It is my intention in the first chapter to offer readers a brief biographical sketch of Lonergan's life and intellectual influences. For those already familiar with Lonergan, this chapter, no doubt, might prove to be too basic. For those who might be unfamiliar with Lonergan's life and work, it is my hope that this brief work might serve as a primer.

In chapter two, I would like to offer an overview of Lonergan's work prior to his writing of *Insight*, especially in his creation of what might be described as *Communal Novum Organon*, as well as his work in understanding the four aspects of dogma in *The Way to Nicea* (1976), as well as a very short introduction to his *magnum opus, Insight: A Study into Human Understanding* (1957).

Chapter three will bring us to a study of what is, in my opinion, the most important work of Lonergan for those who study fundamental theology, namely *Method in Theology* (1972). The fourth and final chapter will begin to discuss what was left undone from Lonergan's work, which can be seen completed in the work of Lonergan's theological heir, Robert Doran, SJ (d. 2021).

Chapter One

Lonergan: A Brief Biography

Bernard Lonergan was born on December 17, 1904 in Buckingham, Quebec, Canada. Gerald Lonergan, his father, was part of a long-settled family of Irish descent living as Anglophones in a predominantly Francophone area. Gerald Lonergan was, by training and profession, an engineer, eventually becoming a land surveyor. His mother, Josephine Wood, was of English descent, and her family arrived in Canada by way of the United States, with her family emigrating at the time of the American Revolution. By all accounts a devout woman, her family had become Catholic two generations before.[1] From his father, Lonergan had learned not only the importance of possessing a mathematical mind,[2] but also the importance of honesty. Bernard Lonergan described his father as "The most honest man I ever met."[3] From his mother, young Lonergan developed two traits which would prove essential in his life: first, a love of God and second, a love of

---

[1] Valentine Rice, "The Lonergans of Buckingham," *Compass* (Journal of the Upper Canada Province of the Society of Jesus, March 1985): 4-5.

[2] The young Lonergan states: "In elementary school I liked math because you know what you had to *do* and could get an answer..." in Pierrot Lambert, Charlotte Tansey, and Cathleen Going, eds., *Caring About Meaning: Patterns in the Life of Bernard Lonergan* (Montreal: Thomas More Institute, 1982), 2 and further "I remember in algebra doing a problem and getting a minus answer. I was sure that I was wrong and I asked, but was told, 'Oh no, that's right. It was the revelation of negative numbers"(Ibid., 133).

[3]Ibid., 40.

culture. Josephine Lonergan was a member of the Dominican Third Order and had a great devotion to the rosary.[4] She also possessed a talent for music and particularly enjoyed Beethoven.[5] Born into a stable and loving family consisting of two other brothers,[6] the young Bernard Lonergan developed a love of learning and a sense of wonder.[7]

The Young Lonergan: Philosophy and Social Concern

Lonergan attended a Jesuit secondary school and junior college at Loyola in Montreal. Quickly, he became immersed in what he would describe in his later writings as a "classicist culture" and the expe-

---

[4] Bernard Lonergan comments: "She joined the Third Order of Saint Dominic and said the beads three times a day for the rest of her life, as far as I know. The Scholastics teaching me at Loyola would come and visit me at the hospital, and they thought she was a very holy woman" (Ibid., 138).

[5] William Mathews, "Lonergan's Apprenticeship," _Lonergan Workshop_ 9, ed. Fred Lawrence (Boston College, 1993), 48; Richard M. Liddy, _Transforming Light: Intellectual Conversion in the Early Lonergan_ (Collegeville, MN: The Liturgical Press, 1993), 3.

[6] Gregory Lonergan followed in his older brother's path and became a Jesuit. The youngest brother, Mark, was an engineer. See Liddy, _Transforming Light_, 4.

[7] The older Lonergan recounts an early episode of wonder in his life: "When I was a boy, I remember being surprised by a companion who assured me that air was real. Astounded, I said, 'No, it's just nothing.' He assured me that 'There's something there, all right. Shake your hand and you will feel it.' So I shook my hand, felt something, and concluded to my amazement that air was real." See Lonergan, "The Natural Theology of _Insight_," (an unpublished paper given at the University of Chicago Divinity School, March 1967), 3, as quoted in Liddy, _Transforming Light_, 4.

rience of living in this culture later offered him the insight that he needed to transcend that particular "cultural matrix."

> When I was sent to boarding school when I was a boy, there were no local high schools- that sort of thing didn't exist, you were sent out to a boarding school- the one I went to in Montreal, in 1918, was organized pretty much along the same lines as Jesuit schools had been since the beginning of the Renaissance, with a few slight modifications. So…I can speak of classical culture as something I was brought up in and gradually learned to move *out* of.[8]

Lonergan, later in life, was rather critical of his Jesuit education. He writes: "At Loyola my acquired habits did not survive my first year: by the mid-terms I was in 3rd High; by the end of the year I was fully aware that the Jesuits did not know how to make one work, that working was unnecessary to pass exams, and that working was regarded by all my fellows as quite anti-social."[9]

---

[8] Bernard Lonergan, "An Interview with Fr. Bernard Lonergan," ed. Philip McShane, in *A Second Collection: Papers by Bernard J. F. Lonergan, S.J.*, eds. W. F. J. Ryan and B. J. Tyrell (Philadelphia: The Westminster Press, 1975), 209-210.

[9] Bernard Lonergan, "Letter of May 5, 1946, to his provincial (John L. Swain)," quoted in Frederick E. Crowe, *Lonergan* (Collegeville, MN: The Liturgical Press, 1992), 5 as well as in Liddy, *Transforming Light*, 6.

Lonergan's Jesuit Vocation

After an illness, Lonergan discerned a religious vocation and entered
the Society of Jesus in 1921. Reflecting on his formation, the older
Lonergan beautifully opines:

> Without any experience of just how and why, one is in the
> state of grace or one recovers it, one leaves all things to follow
> Christ, one binds oneself by vows of poverty, chastity, and
> obedience, one gets through one's daily heavy dose of prayer,
> one longs for the priesthood and later lives by it. Quietly, im-
> perceptibly, there goes forward the transformation operated
> by the *Kurios*, but the delicacy, the gentleness, the deftness,
> of his continual operation in us hides the operation from us.[10]

Receiving the traditional formation that a Jesuit seminarian would
receive in those days, Lonergan learned the importance of self-reflection and the need to purify one's motives through *The Spiritual
Exercises of Saint Ignatius Loyola*. Again, later in life, he would consider the manner in which he was instructed to be a "reduction of St.
Ignatius to decadent conceptualist scholasticism."[11]

---

[10] Bernard Lonergan, "Existenz and Aggiornamento," in *Collection,* in
Collected Works of Bernard Lonergan 4, eds. Frederick E. Crowe and Robert
M. Doran (Toronto: University of Toronto Press, 2005), 230-231.

[11] Lonergan, *Caring About Meaning*, 145. He would also add "…'exam-
ine 'your motives.' When you learn about divine grace you stop worrying
about your motives; someone else is running the ship" (Ibid., 145).

Concerning spiritual formation, Richard Liddy comments that, in the time period in which Lonergan was raised, there was a great fear of illusion in the spiritual life and a definite discouragement of speaking about one's spiritual experiences.[12] Lonergan himself would spend a large part of his later spiritual life rejecting this rigidity, seeking to understand God in a mystical fashion, with love as the entrance way to life in the Divine.[13]

Lonergan's Philosophical Formation

Lonergan was sent to study philosophy at Heythrop College, England and was also given permission to study for a secular degree at the University of London.[14] Affected very much by the overriding fear of rationalism and modernism, the philosophy taught was by and large a Suarezian Neo-Scholastic Thomism, with an emphasis on realism. This realism was based on the notion that a concept is abstracted from one's sense experience and judgment, in turn, returns

---

[12] Liddy, *Transforming Light*, 7.

[13] Lonergan, *Method in Theology*, 290. Liddy comments that there was a breakthrough in Lonergan's prayer life around 1946 (Liddy, *Transforming Light*, 7). Lonergan himself states: "After twenty-four years of aridity in the religious life, I moved into that happy state and have enjoyed it now for over thirty-one years" (Lonergan, "Letter to Louis Roy, August 16, 1977," quoted in Crowe, *Lonergan*, 7).

[14] There are many sources that have studied Lonergan's life and offer an intellectual biography. Among sources consulted for this section include Gerard Whelan, *Redeeming History: Social Concern in Bernard Lonergan and Robert Doran* (Rome: Gregorian and Biblical Press, 2013); Liddy, *Transforming Light* and Crowe, *Lonergan*.

the concept to sensible reality. Present was a unity of sense experience and in intellect, according to the Aristotelian system. Gerald Whelan notes that even the young Lonergan derided this "abstraction of concept from sense experience" as too simplistic and thought the system to be too "conceptualist."[15] "Put in a penny, pull the trigger and the transition from box to matches is spontaneous, immediate and necessary."[16]

Deeply affected intellectually by the Suarezian and neo-scholastic manualism that marked the majority of his philosophical and theological formation, Lonergan began to develop his own theological and philosophical approach, being heavily influenced by thinkers like Plato, Augustine, and John Henry Newman, as well as primary influence, Aquinas. Summarizing his intellectual genealogy, Lonergan writes:

> I had learnt honesty from my teachers of philosophy at Heythrop College. I had had an introduction to modern science from Joseph's *Introduction to Logic* and from the mathematics tutor at Heythrop, Fr. Charles O'Hara. I had become something of an existentialist from my study of Newman's *A Grammar of Assent*. I had become a Thomist through the influence of Maréchal mediated to me by Stefanos Stefanu and through Bernard Leeming's lectures on the *unicum esse in Christo*. In a practical way I had become familiar with

---

[15] Whelan, *Redeeming History,* 16.

[16] Lonergan, "The Syllogism," *Blandyke Papers,* no. 285 (March 1928), 1 quoted in Liddy, *Transforming Light,* 22.

historical work both in my doctoral dissertation on *gratia operans* and in my later study of *verbum* in Aquinas. *Insight* was the fruit of all of this. It enabled me to achieve in myself what since has been called *Die anthropologische Wende*.[17]

Lonergan begins to create his cognitive theory which could best be termed as "discursive." This discursive method, described by Whelan as using the "metaphor of a human conversation or discussion where a number of issues are talked-through before participants agree on a conclusion."[18]

Lonergan, as mentioned before, used his years of philosophical study to also study secular topics like mathematics that later could be used to teach in Jesuit run secondary schools.[19] However, due to his other intellectual pursuits, Lonergan felt that there was at times direct contradiction between his ecclesiastical studies and his secular studies.

Lonergan's Philosophical Influences

In his Heythrop years, Lonergan's discursive cognitive theory developed under his personal study of John Henry Newman, in

---

[17] Bernard Lonergan, "Insight Revisited," in *A Second Collection: Papers by Bernard J.F. Lonergan, S.J.*, eds. W. F. J. Ryan and B. J. Tyrell (Philadelphia: Westminster Press, 1974), 276.

[18] Whelan, *Redeeming History*, 16.

[19] Secondary school teachers, with proper qualification, receive a governmental salary in the United Kingdom. See Whelan, *Redeeming History*, 17.

particular, through his growing appreciation of *An Essay in Aid of a Grammar of Assent*. Newman would state that the ultimate cognitional reference point would be the subject's experience of the dynamics of one's own knowing.[20] In addition, the young Lonergan learned from his study of Newman how to use examples from the Church's tradition as sources for the formation of his own cognitive theory. Another major influence on Lonergan at this point in his life was J.A. Stewart's platonic philosophy, most especially exemplified in Stewart's *Plato's Doctrine of Ideas* (1909). In a very real sense, the budding theologian learned from Stewart the importance of knowing context and the reality of historical consciousness. From Stewart, Lonergan learned that Plato's insights in psychology and philosophy were valid, but had to be transposed to address the growth that had occurred over the centuries.

From his study of Newman, which led him to Stewart's Plato, Lonergan discerned that what is meant by Platonic ideas is actually the sense of wonder in the human subject. Lonergan also found in Plato an important dialogue partner about which was becoming for him a major concern, culture. Liddy writes: "What will become evident in Lonergan's unpublished writings from the mid-thirties is that Plato gave Lonergan the sense of normativeness of intelligence in its own right, a normativeness that in Plato becomes *the* means of cultural critique"[21] and further, "The achievement of Platonism lay in its

---

[20] Whelan comments: "Newman alerted him to the fact that there is something prior to an act of judging truth that involves a mysterious relatedness to God whose light shines through our 'moral as well as our intellectual being'" (Ibid.).

[21] Liddy, *Transforming Light*, 47-48.

power of criticism. The search for a definition of virtue in the earlier dialogues establishes that virtue is a certain something, the emergence of a new light upon experience. The discovery of the idea, of intelligible forms, gave not only dialectic but also the means of social criticism. For it enabled man to express not by symbol but by concept the divine."[22] It is this normativeness that Lonergan would bring into his later analysis of culture. Lonergan writes:

> "Towns and cities will not be happy till philosophers are kings" is the central position of Plato's *Republic*, and the *Republic* is the centre of the dialogues. To Plato, Pericles, the idol of Athenian aspirations, was an idiot; he built docks and brought the fruits of all lands to Athens…but he neglected the one thing necessary, the true happiness of the citizens. For did not the dialectic reveal that no man without self-contradiction could deny that suffering injustice was better than doing injustice, that pain was compatible with happiness, that shame, the interior contradiction, the lie in the soul of a man to himself, was incompatible with happiness.[23]

Later in life, Lonergan became very interested in Eric Voegelin's Platonic interpretations, especially as they pertained to culture. Lonergan stated: "I had always been given the impression that Plato's dialogues were concerned with the pure intellect until I read Dr.

---

[22] Unpublished notes on philosophy of history, available at the Lonergan Research Institute, Toronto, quoted in Ibid., 48.

[23] Unpublished notes on philosophy of history, available at the Lonergan Research Institute, Toronto, as quoted in Ibid.

Voegelin and learned that they were concerned with social decline, the break-up of the Greek city-states. It was human reasonableness trying to deal with an objective social, political mess."[24] In this sense, the task of Lonergan is similar to Plato- using "human reasonableness…to deal with an objective social, political mess."

Lonergan, concerning Plato, writes: "I don't think that he has the answers but certainly he can build up interest and start some serious questions."[25] However, he was troubled by the fact that Plato was more concerned with the act of direct insight than the judgment of truth that was necessary to produce the act.[26] He states: "I got interested in Plato during regency and come to understand him; this left my nominalism quite intact but gave a theory of intellect as well."[27] Naturally enough, this lack in Plato led Lonergan to the work of the neo-Platonist, Augustine of Hippo. From Augustine, Lonergan retrieved a notion on how insight leads the subject to the affirmation of truth, as well as a Christian understanding of the Divine as the object of knowing and that the desire to know the good and true in

---

[24] Lonergan, quoted in *The Question as Commitment: A Symposium*, edited by E. Cahn and C. Going (Montreal: The Thomas More Institute, 1977), 119.

[25] Lonergan, *Caring About Meaning*, 49. Liddy notes that in the mid-1930s the Platonic dialogues were among the few books that Lonergan actually owned. Lonergan, in time, gave up his study of Plato, and stated: "I had other fish to fry" (Liddy, *Transforming Light*, 47; Lonergan, *Caring About Meaning*, 48).

[26] Whelan, *Redeeming History*, 18. See also Liddy, *Transforming Light*, 49.

[27] Bernard Lonergan, "Letter to Provincial, Henry Keane, January 22, 1935," quoted in Liddy, *Redeeming History*, 49.

created reality is an indication of the presence of the Divine within us.[28]

Lonergan's Theological Formation

For his theological formation, Lonergan was sent to study at the Pontifical Gregorian University, Rome. Ordained to the priesthood in 1937, he completed his doctoral work in 1940 with his thesis, *Gratia Operans: Study of the Speculative Development of St. Thomas Aquinas*.[29] His "eleven-year apprenticeship to St. Thomas Aquinas," was fruitful, bearing his work on cognitional theory in Aquinas, which would, in fact, be essential for his later major work in *Insight: A Study in Human Understanding*.[30]

Lonergan's Theological Influences

During his studies at the Gregorian University, Lonergan was able to rediscover the importance of Aquinas after stripping the *Doctor Communis* of all the Suarezian residue that had accumulated over

---

[28] Whelan, *Redeeming History*, 19.

[29] The dissertation was later published as *Grace and Freedom: Operative Grace in the Thought of St. Thomas Aquinas*, in *Collected Works of Bernard Lonergan* 1, eds. Frederick E. Crowe and Robert M. Doran(Toronto: University of Toronto Press, 2000).

[30] Lonergan's work in cognitive theory would be published as a series of five articles in *Theological Studies* in the years 1946-1949. These articles would later be published in collected form as *Verbum: Word and Idea in Aquinas*, in *Collected Works of Bernard Lonergan* 2, eds. Frederick E. Crowe and Robert M. Doran(Toronto: University of Toronto Press, 1997).

the years. This rediscovery occurred through three Jesuits Thomists: Peter Hoenen, Joseph Maréchal and Leo W. Keeler.[31] From Hoenen, Lonergan learned to return to what Thomas Aquinas had actually written and not to simply rely on the interpretations of the neo-scholastics, who in a very real sense attributed the thought of the nominalist John Duns Scotus to his polar opposite, Thomas Aquinas.[32]

From Joseph Maréchal, Lonergan, although never an actual classroom student of this Belgian professor, learned the value of interdisciplinary Thomistic research. Maréchal's familiarity with modern psychology added an extra dimension to the study of Thomism. One of the major contributions of Joseph Maréchal to Thomism was the inclusion of the thought of contemporary philosophers and concepts, like Kant's "transcendental turn to the subject." From this point, Lonergan's cognitive theory, one based on a discursive method, gains more credence by stating that "knowing is more than just taking a good look."[33]

---

[31] See Whelan, *Redeeming History*, 20-26.

[32] See Ibid.,21 and Liddy, *Transforming Light*, 94. Lonergan writes: "Scotus posits concepts first, then the apprehension of nexus between concepts...while for Aquinas understanding precedes conceptualization which is rational, for Scotus, understanding is preceded by conceptualization which is a matter of metaphysical mechanics" (Liddy, *Transforming Light*, 93 quoting Lonergan, *Verbum*, 25n-26).

[33] Whelan summarizes the thought of Michael Vertin on the connection of Joseph Maréchal and Bernard Lonergan. He quotes Vertin: "Lonergan unreservedly endorses Maréchal's contention that I have my notion of being in general, my idea of all reality, by nature rather than by acquisition...it only prefigures being in its determinate plenitude" and "Lonergan also vigorously embraces the most prominent element in Maréchal's account of how I know particular beings. The culminating step of the process

Finally, Lonergan was influenced in his re-appreciation of Aquinas through his reading of Leo Keeler. From Keeler, Lonergan learned that in the discursive process of human knowing, it was necessary to distinguish between a cognitive level of insight and judgment level.[34] In the course of his studies, Lonergan came to what could be later called in his terminology his intellectual conversion. In the course of writing a letter to his superior in January 1935, Lonergan, after some years of deep emotions and much reflection, confidently declared: "I am certain (and I am not one who becomes certain easily) that I can put together a Thomistic metaphysic of history."[35] He can do so by working through a level of self-reflection, beginning with "an initial Cartesian cogito." This turn to the subject would prove to be an essential element in Lonergan's cognitive theory that will be more fully discussed next chapter.[36]

---

is never a matter of confrontation, perception, taking a good look- on the contrary, [it] always culminates with judging, where judging is posited, asserting, affirming. (Michael Vertin, "The Finality of Human Spirit: From Maréchal to Lonergan," *Lonergan Workshop* 19, "Celebrating the 450th Jesuit Jubilee," ed. Fred Lawrence (Boston: Boston College, 2006), 275 As quoted in Whelan, *Redeeming History*, 23 n.18)

[34] Whelan, *Redeeming History*, 23-24; Liddy, *Transforming Light*, 96-100.

[35] Lonergan, "Letter of January 22, 1935," 4-5 as quoted in Liddy, *Transforming Light*, 110.

[36] Lonergan, "Letter of January 22, 1935," 4 as quoted in Liddy, *Transforming Light*,110; Whelan, *Redeeming History*, 26. Lonergan writes: "The current interpretation of St. Thomas is a consistent misinterpretation- From an initial Cartesian *"cogito"* I can work out a luminous and unmistakable meaning to *intellectus agens et posibilis*, abstraction, conversion to phantasm, etc., etc. The [neo-Scholastic] Thomists cannot even give a

Lonergan's Growing Social Concern

While Lonergan was growing in his own intellectual conversion, he was also growing in his social concern and awareness. Influenced by papal encyclicals like Leo XIII's *Rerum Novarum* (1891) and Pius XI's *Quadragesimo Anno* (1932) as well as the reality of worldwide events like the Great Depression, Lonergan was acutely aware of the reality of poverty. He writes: "The political economists are utterly discredited: no economist today believes in the old theories; no thinking man who has lived through the Depression can accept the view that the great happiness of the greatest number results automatically from the laws of supply and demand."[37] Influenced by his studies in Heythrop under the rare non-Suarezian Lewis Watt, Lonergan learned that economic theory must be part of any wider philosophy of history.[38] The young Jesuit also studied at the University of London where he learned the work of empiricist philosophers like Bertrand Russell and John Stewart Mill and saw in their work a demonstration that mathematics and the natural sciences had a tremendous

---

meaning to most of this...I can put together a Thomistic metaphysic of history that will throw Hegel and Marx, despite the enormity of their influence on this account, into the shade" (Lonergan, "Letter of January 22, 1935," 4-5 as quoted in Liddy, *Transforming Light*, 110).

[37] Lonergan, as quoted in William Mathew, *Lonergan's Quest: A Study of Desire in the Authoring of Insight* (Toronto: University of Toronto Press, 2005), 111.

[38] Watt also introduced his students to the thought of Karl Marx as well as the papal social encyclicals, thus solidifying in the young Lonergan's mind the need to know and appreciate contemporary philosophy. See Mathew, *Lonergan's Quest*, 33, 42-43 and Whelan, *Redeeming History*, 28.

impact on questions of epistemology and metaphysics, eventually influencing Lonergan's philosophy of history. From his studies of J.A.
Stewart's Platonic theory, Lonergan grew in understanding of the
role of virtue in the citizens in the creation of a just society.[39]

One final major influence on Lonergan was the historian Christopher Dawson. In his attempt to ascertain how present-day Western
civilization could learn from ancient cultures, Dawson suggested an
empiricist method that did not read into the older cultures contemporary values and mores.[40] Lonergan commented that "Christopher
Dawson's *The Age of the Gods* introduced me to my hitherto normative or classicist notion."[41]

Lonergan and Economics

Much of the work, such as his concept of dialectic, his philosophy
of history, and his cognitive theory, pursued by Lonergan in the late
1930s and 1940s will be discussed more fully in chapter two. Lonergan spent his early years teaching in the French-speaking Jesuit
theologate, *Marie Immaculée* in Montreal, eventually being trans-
ferred to the Jesuits' theologate in Toronto. For the sake of brevity, it
is sufficient to state that his growing philosophy of history and his
social concern led him to create a theory of macroeconomics.

---

[39] Liddy, *Transforming Light*, 48; Whelan, *Redeeming History*, 29.

[40] See Christopher Dawson, *The Age of the Gods* (1928). Reissued by
Catholic University of America Press, 2012.

[41] Lonergan, "Insight Revisited," 264.

Lonergan's "An Essay in Circulation Analysis,"[42] William Mathews notes that Lonergan considered this work in macroeconomics the second part of the work he had begun with his philosophy of history. He also mentions that prior to working on the actual essay, Lonergan wrote a four-page schema of his ideas (around 1940-1941) for the essay, signifying why he would wish to undertake this study in economics. The main reason why Lonergan branched out of his theological pursuits to investigate macroeconomic theory was to study how economics progresses and declines and, in the acquiring of this knowledge, to aid societies in avoiding tragedies like the Great Depression in the future. Many of the ideas that Lonergan would develop in *Insight* are first articulated here. What is needed is a patient adherence to one's own cognition. Mathews comments:

> Economic production is also for Lonergan a series of conditioned emergences, the emergent component of what he will later call emergent probability: 'In making a coat of mail each new link has to be added to previous links, and similarly the successive stages of economic progress presuppose the previous stages and arise from them.' Each stage having emerged, there is the challenge of survival, and so in time the stagecoach gives way to the train, clipper ships to steamers, money

---

[42] Bernard Lonergan, *Macroeconomic Dynamics: an Essay in circulation Analysis*, in *Collected Works of Bernard Lonergan* 15, eds. Patrick Byrne, Frederick Lawrence, and Charles Hefling Jr. (Toronto: University of Toronto, 2005).

changers give way to brokers who in turn give way to banks and financiers.[43]

The one who is charged with analyzing the economic systems himself or herself has to be intellectually converted so that he or she can be able to respond to the changes that inevitably will occur. The economic analyst needs to be aware that knowledge is more than just "taking a good look." Having a proper cognitive theory is essential in the creation of a just economy. The flow of services and goods is of primary importance to Lonergan and he sees that this is where governments can assist their citizens concretely. Money flow is involved in this process. Whelan summarizes Lonergan's thought:

> Lonergan identifies two ways in which this involvement occurs: the first involves the way money exercises a kind of direct "oiling of the wheels" of production, consumption, and exchange in an economy. This ordinary use of money includes paying salaries to workers who produce goods that they can themselves buy.[44]

Money is also involved in the creation of new products and technology that can aid in the production of goods. Investment must play an important role in the stability of an economy. According to Lonergan, there are four key phases in an economy:

---

[43] Mathew, *Lonergan's Quest*, 115, as quoted in Whelan, *Redeeming History*, 41.

[44] Whelan, *Redeeming History*, 42.

...a capitalist phase that transforms the means of production;
a materialist phase that exploits new ideas to raise the standard of living; a cultural phase that turns material well-being
and power to equipping the developing cultural pursuits; a
static phase in which the process lies fallow and non-eco-
nomic activity develops independently of material conditions...[45]

At the essence, Lonergan was seeking "a stable and permanent solution for the monetary requirements of a long-term expansion."[46]
Lonergan also created a system for governments, who bore the primary responsibility for safe economic system to regulate economy
that involves different levels of taxation and interest rates.

Lonergan and Pastoral Theology

It is during this time period that Lonergan decided to publish his
Verbum articles for publication in the newly formed *Theological
Studies*, edited by John Courtney Murray. At the same time, Lonergan was also involved in discussion of practical matters like his
apostolate at the Thomas More Center in Montreal, which primarily
involved adult education classes in theology as well as in his work as
an essayist in a local Catholic magazine, *The Montreal Beacon*. All

---

[45] Lonergan, *For a New Political Economy*, in *Collected Works of Bernard Lonergan* 15, ed. Philip J. McShane (Toronto: University of Toronto,
2005), 27 as quoted in Mathews, *Lonergan's Quest*, 115.
[46] Lonergan, *For a New Political Economy*, 100 as quoted in Mathews,
Lonergan's Quest, 121.

this is mentioned to exemplify the "polyphonic interests"[47] in which Lonergan was engaged.

Lonergan, Rejection and Redemption

In 1947, Lonergan underwent what was described by Mathews as his "year of crisis." This "year of crisis" occurred in no small part by emotion and physical problems accentuated by his transfer from Montreal to a new English speaking theologate in Toronto.[48] However, another mitigating factor for his difficulties was the rejection of his 1943 article "Finality, Love, Marriage." The editor of the magazine in which the article was published wrote that Lonergan's article directly contradicted the teaching of the Catholic Church concerning marriage. This accusation caused Lonergan great personal pain, but, nonetheless, he continued to believe that the Church was basing itself on philosophy that could not fully comprehend all the issues at hand. However, as a loyal son of the Church and of Saint Ignatius, he remained silent and did not address these accusations.[49] While in no way undergoing the same level of persecution that his American

---

[47] This metaphor, "polyphonic interests" is used by Mathews to refer to the years 1940-1947. Gerard Whelan extends the time period to include Lonergan's years of doctoral studies (1938-1940).

[48] See Mathews, "A creative illness," in *Lonergan's Quest*, 185-90 and Whelan, "Emotional Problems," in *Redeeming History*, 52.

[49] See Mathews, *Lonergan's Quest*, 128; Whelan, *Redeeming History*, 53.

Jesuit confrere John Courtney Murray suffered, this criticism and some others caused Lonergan great pain.[50]

In 1948, Lonergan underwent a kind of spiritual conversion, commenting years later "After twenty-four years of aridity in religious life, I moved into that happier state and have enjoyed it for over thirty-one years now."[51] Whelan comments:

> ...Lonergan also achieved a moment of clarity about how to understand his intellectual vocation. He now recognized that his real passion was to clarify the kind of philosophical questions he had always recognized as being foundational to an effective social concern. He now confirmed some decision he had already been making more informally during the proceeding years to sideline a series of interests- in a philosophy of history, a theology of marriage, and in macroeconomics- and to concentrate on the line of enquiry he had begun with the first of his *Verbum* articles.[52]

Lonergan in Rome

From 1953-1965, Lonergan taught at the Pontifical Gregorian University, Rome, until he returned, due to health concerns to

---

[50] Mathews details a critique of his *Verbum* articles in *Modern Schoolman* by Jesuit scholastic Matthew J. O'Connell as well as a rejection on the part of some economists of his "An Essay in Circulation Analysis" (Mathews, *Lonergan's Quest*, 182-184; 130).

[51] Ibid.,189.

[52] Whelan, *Redeeming History*, 55.

Canada. As a professor of dogmatic theology at the Pontifical Gregorian University, he was exposed to students from all around the world. The universality, the catholicity of the Church was apparent to him. He realized that it was necessary for him, as a professor who wanted to engage with his students and to communicate the doctrine of the Church, as well as his own concepts articulated in *Insight*, to continue his own study.

In 1953, the world, internationally, was still reeling from the horrors of the Second World War and the rise of atheistic communism. The Church, in the pontificate of Pius XII was processing the importance of *Humanae Generis* (1950) and the impact that it had on theology in general and theologians in particular.[53] Intellectually, Lonergan's students at the Gregorian were engaging philosophically with phenomenology and existentialism as well as having a growing interest in hermeneutics.[54] Describing this time period, Lonergan

---

[53] It should be noted that this is the same time period that John Courtney Murray in the United States was working out his theories of Church and State relations. The Holy Office, under Alfredo Cardinal Ottaviani, was in a contentious relationship with several theologians, among them Karl Rahner, Henri de Lubac and John Courtney Murray.

[54] As a professor of dogmatic theology during the academic year, Lonergan was pleased to offer in the summer months several "Summer Institutes" throughout the United States and Canada. This permitted him to engage, in his dialectic method, existentialist, hermeneutical and phenomenological thinkers. Gerard Whelan writes: "Lonergan engaged with these authors in a two-step manner. First he identifies both positions and counterpositions in their thought; next he attempts to develop the positions in these authors by undertaking a shift to intentionality analysis within his own thinking on subjectivity and history" (Whelan, *Redeeming History*, 106). The fruits of these summer lectures are found in *Phenomenology and*

writes: " For the first ten years I was there I lectured in alternative years on the Incarnate Word and on the Trinity to both second and third year theologians. They were about six hundred and fifty strong and between them, not individually but distributively, they seemed to read everything. It was quite a challenge."[55] Professionally, as an academic, he was on the threshold of publishing what is considered by most to be his greatest work, *Insight: A Study in Human Under-standing.*[56] Throughout this entire time period, Lonergan himself was become increasingly converted, intellectually, morally, and spiritually. Lonergan, in this time period (1953-1965), also offered a seminar for graduate students at the Gregorian in theological method.[57]

Logic, in *Collected Works of Bernard Lonergan* 18, ed. Philip McShane (Toronto: University of Toronto Press, 2001), in which Lonergan attempted to engage the thought of Edmund Husserl; *Topics in Education*, in *Collected Works of Bernard Lonergan* 10, eds. Frederick Crowe and Robert Doran (Toronto: University of Toronto, 1993) began as a series of lectures to Catholic high school teachers in which, among other topics, Lonergan discusses the thought of Martin Heidegger.

[55] Lonergan, "Insight Revisited,"276.

[56] It is beyond the scope of this text to discuss the monumental impact that *Insight*, in *Collected Works of Bernard Lonergan* 3, eds. Frederick Crowe and Robert Doran (Toronto: University of Toronto Press, 1992) had on cognitive theory and influenced Lonergan's later works, like *Method in Theology*. *Insight* also had a tremendous impact on Lonergan himself. He later writes: "To say it all with the greatest brevity: one has not only to read *Insight* but also to discover oneself in oneself." (Lonergan, *Method in Theology*, 260).

[57] Gerard Whelan notes that these graduate seminars were not offered in the faculty of theology, but in the philosophy faculty "…where, it seems, more creative thought was possible than within the theology department"

The Later Lonergan: Social Concern Again Evident

In February 1965, Lonergan began to come to the insight of functional specialties. In June 1965, while visiting Canada and undergoing a routine medical examination, Lonergan was diagnosed with
lung cancer, and, for reasons both physical and emotional, it was determined by his superiors that he would leave his teaching position
at the Gregorian University and remain in Canada, as a research professor at Regis College, Toronto.[58]

His illness left him in a much weaker state, and Lonergan's work
on the functional specialties took him much longer than he had originally anticipated. The article on functional specialties was finally
published in 1969 in the *Gregorianum* and was adapted to become
Method in Theology's Chapter 5, "Functional Specialization."[59] As a
research professor at Boston College, Lonergan produced *Method in
Theology* (1972), a culmination of his desire to create a theological
method for Christian theology. In November 1984, Lonergan died in

----

(Whelan, *Redeeming History*, 129). By and large, Lonergan's lectures at the
Gregorian University were limited to teaching first-cycle students in dogmatic theology, where the curriculum was already predetermined.

[58] It should be noted that Lonergan had already taught at this institu-
tion from 1947-1953 and, in this return to Regis College, he was given a
very limited teaching schedule. In terms of his health, Lonergan chose to
delay an operation to remove his lung, as he wished to develop his concept
of the functional specialties. After the primary operation, he was required
to have a secondary operation and eventually was declared cancer-free.

[59] See Bernard Lonergan, "Functional Specialties in Theology," *Gregorianum* 50 (1969):485-504.

his native Canada. Frederick Crowe, in the homily given at the funeral mass of Bernard Lonergan, said:

> Writing of the good choices and actions that make us what we are, he (Lonergan) calls them "the work of the free and responsible agent producing the first and only edition of himself"...that is a book I and each one of us must write alone as we go through life, producing day by day a new paragraph to achieve the first and only edition of myself...The one and only work that really mattered was the work of which he wrote last Monday morning the final paragraph, and turned it over to his maker for censorship and- we have not the slightest doubt- for divine approval.[60]

Few outside theological circles might recognize the impact that Lonergan had accomplished in his lifetime, most especially through his works, *Insight* and *Method in Theology*, but in his own self-actualization, Lonergan offers all who strive to practice the science and art of theology the challenge of the Delphic oracle- "Know Thyself." Only through a four-fold conversion, intellectual, moral, spiritual, and psychic can one truly offer to the Church and the culture a theology that is authentic and true.

---

[60] Frederick E. Crowe, "Homily at the Funeral of Bernard Lonergan," (Given at Our Lady of Lourdes Church, Toronto, Canada, on November 29, 1984 and originally published in *Compass: A Jesuit Journal*, special issue honoring Bernard Lonergan, S.J., 1904-1984 (March, 1985): 21-23) in Frederick E. Crowe, *Appropriating the Lonergan Idea*, ed. Michael Vertin (Washington, D.C.: The Catholic University of America Press, 1989), 389.

Chapter Two

Pre-*Insight* and *Insight*

Lonergan, as mentioned in chapter one, served as a professor of dogmatic theology at the Gregorian University for many years. As such, he would publish a *dispense* for his students, a small guide written in Latin, which would give his students an outline of his course material. This would have been helpful to the large number of students, from the many countries in the world, now in Rome, learning in Latin, while sitting in a large aula. For the baccalaureate courses in theology at the Gregorian, the professor would lecture and the students would take notes, all culminating in a ten-minute oral exam in which the professor could ask the student a question on any of the material covered in the class. *The Way to Nicaea* (1976) is a translation of this *dispense*. What the reader discovers in the text is the application of Lonergan's theological method to the Trinitarian questions raised at the Council of Nicaea (325 AD).

The Preface of The Way to Nicaea

Lonergan divided his class on the Trinity into two sections: the first was a dogmatic part, of which *The Way to Nicaea* is the translation; the second was a systematic part. After an introductory preface, Lonergan goes to explain the difference between the aim, the proper object and method of dogmatic theology as opposed to positive theology. He states: "Dogmatic development, viewed in its totality, has four main aspects: an objective, a subjective, an evaluative and a hermeneutical aspect."[1]

The Objective Aspect of Dogma

The objective aspect is derived from a comparison between the gospels and apostolic writings, which are truth and which seek to "penetrate the sensibility, fire the imagination, engage the affections, touch the heart, open the eyes, attract and impel the will of the reader,"[2] and conciliar statements, which are designed to be clear, and objects, "bypassing the senses."[3] Therefore, in terms of the objective aspect, the theologian must learn to transition between two very different forms of literature, as scripture is designed for the whole person, and conciliar documents are meant solely for the intellect. He or she must also learn, objectively, that scriptures address all truth and the conciliar documents address only a single truth.

The Subjective Aspect of Dogma

Subjectively, in reading scripture and in reading conciliar documents, the subject must have an interior change in himself or herself. Lonergan makes a distinction between differentiated and undifferentiated consciousness. The undifferentiated consciousness involves

---

[1] Bernard Lonergan, *The Way to Nicea: The Dialectical Development of Trinitarian Theology*, trans. Conn O'Donovan from the first part of *De Deo Trino*, (Philadelphia: The Westminster Press, 1976), 1.

[2] Ibid.

[3] Ibid.

the whole person in his entirety; the differentiated consciousness operates on a single level. Describing the differentiated consciousness, Lonergan writes:

> ...the scientist, or the speculative thinker, tends towards a goal that is not that of the whole man, but only of his intellect. The will is therefore restricted to willing the good of the intellect, which is the truth; imagination throws up only those images that induce understanding or suggest a judgment; feelings and emotions, finally, are as if anaesthetized, so firmly are they kept in control.[4]

For Lonergan, scripture corresponds to the undifferentiated consciousness and magisterial, conciliar documents correspond to the differentiated consciousness. The theologian must learn to make a "transition from undifferentiated common sense...to the intellectual pattern of experience."[5]

The Evaluative Aspect of Dogma

Lonergan also describes the evaluative aspect of dogmatic development. This evaluative aspect occurs not only in a manner purely objective, but one that is also subjective. It is necessary for the theologian to subordinate his or her powers to the intellect in order to

---

[4] Ibid., 3.
[5] Ibid.

achieve that "clarity and precision that is proper to the intellectual life."[6] Lonergan states:

> ...those who have made some progress in the intellectual life, therefore, and can move with ease into the intellectual pattern of experience, find nothing more clear and precise than the meaning of a geometrical theorem or a dogmatic definition. On the other hand, when intellect acts as just one among many diverse powers- and this applies to most people most of the time- then less attention is focussed (*sic*) on the proper end of the intellect. In ordinary every-day living there is much that is taken for granted as being sufficiently clear; what is thus taken for granted may be described and stated in detail, from many different angles, but it is so tied to particular circumstances, so embedded in the intentions of individual people, that it can never be reduced to the clarity of a definition or a theorem.[7]

Lonergan warns his readers not to glorify the undifferentiated consciousness of early cultures like the Hebrews. As culture progresses, becoming more and more highly diversified and specialized, so too must religion. It is the function of dogmas to render differentiated consciousness religious. The religious aspects of one's life must develop intellectually and, with a differentiated consciousness, the

---

[6] Ibid., 5
[7] Ibid.

"whole tenor and direction of life" will change.[8] Lonergan states: "And so if one argues that there is nothing religious about intellect, one is not serving the cause of true religion, but rather that of secularism."[9]

The Hermeneutical Aspect of Dogma

The fourth aspect of dogma is hermeneutical. Citing the Thomistic axiom, "…whatever is received, is received after the manner of the receiver," Lonergan states that the human mind "imposes unity on the contents," assuring a natural selection which leads to an initial structuring which in turn, "anticipates future judgments."[10] One must be truly converted to make a correct apprehension of data. If one is working from a false or erroneous epistemology, cognitional theory, or metaphysics, the apprehension of the data received will be faulty.

The Truth of the Revealed Word of God

In order to correctly understand dogma, one must start from the point of view that it comes forth from the revealed word of God, as set forth in the Church's tradition. The word of God is true, and without this as the primary basis of comprehension, one will have an incorrect interpretation. Lonergan warns: "…it is not enough to attend

---

[8] Ibid., 6.
[9] Ibid., 6-7.
[10] Ibid., 7.

to the word of God as true, if one has a false conception of the relationship between truth and reality. Reality is known through true judgment; explicit knowledge of this fact, however, is a difficult attainment and is proportionately rare."[11]

One's consciousness needs to be differentiated, and each differentiated consciousness is bound by different, unique horizons, but truth is truth. The truth expressed in different horizons is merely a "different expression of the same truth."[12] Lonergan states that there is no radical discontinuity between dogma and scripture, and that, ultimately, the one thing necessary is to hold to the truth that is the word of God.

The Interlocking Relationship between the Four Aspects of Dogma

Each aspect of dogma relates one to the other, according to Lonergan. In dogmatic development, the objective aspect, presuming intellectual conversion on the part of the interlocutors, can "prescind from all the other components or features of interpersonal communication."[13] The evaluative aspect arises out of the objective and subjective aspects, coming from the reality that one not only act but also reflect and judge. Finally, the hermeneutical aspect of dogma is related to the evaluative aspect in the sense that one must know the horizon out of which the dogma is arising, and this includes knowledge of the historical circumstances.

---

[11] Ibid., 8-9.
[12] Ibid.,10.
[13] Ibid., 11.

An understanding of Lonergan's concept of the development of dogma is essential for an understanding of the accomplishment of the Second Vatican Council. The historically conscious, intellectually differentiated individual must have insight, understanding, and judgment, taking into account the objective, subjective, evaluative, and hermeneutical aspects of dogma. And, above all else, the interpreter of dogma must be a person of faith, faith in the truth that is the divinely revealed word of God, as given to the Church through tradition.

Insight as Background for Theological Method

In his text, *Insight: A Study of Human Understanding*, Lonergan deals with cognitive structure. *Insight* largely expands on Lonergan's work in *Verbum*. Lonergan does not have many novel additions to his earlier work but offers a clarification of his own thought that comes from the maturity of his research and reading. Working out of his Thomistic roots, challenged by his students' interest in contemporary philosophy, *Insight* offers Lonergan's clearest explanations of the levels of consciousness. As in all of Lonergan's thought, it is an invitation to go deeper, to not remain on the surface level, but to explore what it means to be the knower and to know how and what is knowable.

According to Lonergan, there are three, self-structuring, and functionally interrelated cognitional levels. On the first level, there is data. It is the level of perception, of free images, of utterances as expression. It is the level of realizing that there is something to be understood. It is the level of the what, why, how often? One cannot remain on this level, but instead, he or she must delve deeper. The pure desire to know makes demands on the knower that cannot be satisfied on this level. It is the level of experience.

The second level offers questions for intelligence. It is the level of insights and formulations, with concepts, images and symbols as the expression of these insights. It is the level of the *quid sit*. It is wondering what exactly are the nature and the state of this thing/concept/etc. Is it clear and distinct? These insights are all on the level of direct understanding. But even this level is not enough for the knower. He or she must still dive deeper, going from understanding that insight to the third level, that of reflecting on that insight. The knower, having grasped the phantasm and formed an insight now knows the insight. But he or she must go deeper.

The third level is the level of critical reflection. It builds upon the second level natural *an sit* question, ultimately asking "Is it true?" This is the level of reflective consciousness and calls us to the level of judgment. This is the level of discovering truth and falsehood and the level where one is called to make a personal commitment. Each of these three levels presupposes and complements the next. There can be no reductionism, no moving backwards, no falling from one level to that of the prior. This level of reflective insight also involves a moral dimension- prior to making a statement, the one who makes a judgment has to make an act of intellectual morality. One must be willing to risk his or her reputation, and one's very credibility when positing a judgment. Terry J. Tekippe phrases this bluntly: "Never make a judgment that outruns the evidence."[14]

History, Progress, and Decline

This call to intellectual honesty is a hallmark of Lonergan's later *Method in Theology*. Lonergan posits two vectors in history: progress and decline. As Raymond Lafontaine notes, Lonergan is "working out the theological implications of his cognitive theory…that 'insight into insight,' leading to the gradual emergence of 'higher viewpoints,' is the motor driving the cumulative process of 'human *progress*.' 'Insight into oversight,' in contrast, is the key to understanding the cumulative progress of *decline*."[15] Lonergan writes:

Insight into insight brings to light the cumulative process of progress. For concrete situations give rise into insights which issue into policies and courses of action. Action transforms the existing situation to give rise to further insights, better policies, more effective courses of actions. It follows that if insight occurs, it keeps recurring; and at each recurrence,

---

[14] Terry J. Tekippe, *What is Lonergan Up to in Insight?: A Primer* (Collegeville, MN: The Liturgical Press, 1996), 80.

[15] Raymond Lafontaine, *The Development of a Moral Doctrine: Religious Liberty and Doctrinal Development in the Works of John Henry Newman and John Courtney Murray*, Excerpta ex Dissertatione ad Doctoratum in Facultate Theologiae Pontificae Universitatis Gregoriane, Romae, (2001), 42.

knowledge develops, action increases its scope, and situations improve.[16]

Decline, on the other hand, is the result of the "finalistic tension of psyche and spirit in consciousness."[17] Lonergan writes in explanation:

> Just as insight can be desired, so too it can be unwanted. Besides the love of light, there can be a love of darkness. If prepossessions and prejudices notoriously vitiate theoretical investigations, much more easily can elementary passions bias understanding in practical and personal matters.[18]

This bias works on three levels. In the individual, it is called "dramatic bias." Dramatic bias functions on an unconscious level and can lead an individual to incorrectly interpret situations and suffer a form of cognitive distortion. The second form of bias is called "individual bias" and involves a conscious decision "to resist the transcendent pull of conscience and to favour egoistic interests."[19]

---

[16] Bernard Lonergan, *Insight: A Study of Human Understanding*, in *Collected Works of Bernard Lonergan* 3, eds. Frederick E. Crowe and Robert M. Doran (Toronto: University of Toronto Press, 1991), 8.

[17] Whelan, *Redeeming History*, 90.

[18] Lonergan, *Insight*, 214.

[19] Whelan, *Redeeming History*, 90. Lonergan describes egoism in the following fashion: "Egoism is neither mere spontaneity nor pure intelligence but an interference of spontaneity with the development of intelligence. With remarkable acumen one solves one's own problems. With startling modesty one does not venture to raise the relevant further questions,

Lonergan states that this bias, which inevitably leads to decline, is not only in the individual, but also is present in social structures. With bluntness, he describes this form of bias in the following manner: "Unfortunately, as insight and oversight commonly are mated, so also are progress and decline. We reinforce our love of truth with a practicality that is equivalent to an obscurantism. We correct old evils with a passion that mars the new good. We are not pure. We compromise."[20]

Dialectic and Cosmopolis

Lonergan states that it is necessary, if one wishes to be an authentic person, to promote progress and to reverse decline, it is essential to employ a method of dialectic.[21] Dialectic method holds that

---

Can one's solution be generalized? Is it compatible with the social order that exists? Is it compatible with any social order that proximately or even remotely is possible?" (Lonergan, *Insight*, 245).

[20] Lonergan, *Insight*, 91. Lonergan goes on to describe two different sorts of bias that are present in the social realm: the first, "group bias," is expressed in the gathering of "functional groups," and these groups can lead to a class society, structured not only on social function, but also on social success. The second, "general bias," is a refusal of common sense people to admit differing viewpoints. This is much more serious, according to Lonergan, and "What is worse, the deteriorating situation seems to provide the uncritical, biased mind with factual evidence in which the bias is claimed to be verified. So in ever increasing measure intelligence comes to be regarded as irrelevant to practical living" (Ibid., 8).

[21] By genetic method, Lonergan means "the development, or genesis, of new schemes of recurrences either within living things or in the emergence of new living things, one from the other" (Whelan, *Redeeming*

"position," which comes about from authentic reasoning and decid-ing, needs to be developed, and, "counterposition," which arises from the effects of bias, needs to be reversed.[22] By definition, position is "any philosophic pronouncement on any epistemological, metaphys-ical, ethical, or theological issue…" that is "coherent with the basic positions on the real, on knowing, and on objectivity."[23]

Culture needs to cultivate "cosmopolis," namely a "dialectical at-titude of will."[24] Lonergan writes:

> What is both unnecessary and disastrous is the exaltation of the practical, the supremacy of the state, the cult of the class. What is necessary is a cosmopolis that is neither class nor state, that stands above all their claims, that cuts them down to size, that is founded on the native detachment and disin-terestedness of every intelligence, that commands man's first allegiance, that implements itself primarily through that

---

History, 79). See Lonergan, *Insight*, 289ff concerning the human being and genetic method.

[22] Lonergan states that a basic position is present "…if the real is the concrete universe of being and not a subdivision of the 'already out there now" and "if objectivity is conceived as a consequence of intelligent inquiry and critical reflection, and not as a property of vital anticipation, extrover-sion, and satisfaction." On the other hand, a basic counterposition arises "…if it contradicts one or more of the basic positions…" (Lonergan, *Insight*, 413ff)

[23] Ibid., 413.

[24] Ibid., 721.

allegiance, that is too universal to be bribed, too impalpable to be forced, too effective to be ignored.[25]

The only way to live in a world that opposes the very notion of cosmopolis is to develop himself or herself as a truly authentic human being. Lonergan writes:

> The solution has to be a still higher integration of human living. For the problem is radical and permanent; it is independent of the underlying physical, chemical, organic, and psychic manifolds; it is not met by revolutionary change, nor by human discovery, nor by the enforced implementation of discovery; it is as large as human living and human history. Further, the solution has to take people just as they are.[26]

It is precisely this call to authenticity that is necessary for the theologian to embrace in his or her own personal journey that lies at the root of a true method in theology. Lonergan writes:

The crucial issue is an experimental issue, and the experiment will be performed not publicly but privately. It will consist in one's own rational self-consciousness clearly and distinctly taking possession of itself as rational self-consciousness. Up to that decisive achievement all leads. From it all follows. No one else, no matter what his knowledge or his

---

[25] Ibid., 263.
[26] Ibid., 655.

eloquence, no matter what his logical rigor or his persuasiveness, can do it for you…[27]

Personal commitment is essential for the theologian to the process of theology, if it is to be authentic. Lonergan, in *Method in Theology*, writes:

Despite the doubts and denials of positivists and behaviorists, no one, unless some of his organs are deficient, is going to say that never in his life did he have the experience of seeing or of hearing, of touching or smelling or tasting, of imagining or perceiving, of feeling or moving; or that if he appeared to have such experience, still it was mere appearance, since all his life long he has gone about like a somnambulist without any awareness of his own activities. Again, how rare is the man that will preface his lectures by repeating his conviction that never did he have even a fleeting experience of intellectual curiosity, of inquiry, of striving and coming to understand, of expressing what he has grasped by understanding. Rare too is the man that begins his contributions to periodical literature by reminding his potential readers that never in his life did he experience anything that might be called critical reflection, that he never paused about the truth or falsity of any statement, that if ever he seemed to exercise his rationality by passing judgment strictly in accord with the available evidence, then that must be counted mere

---

[27] Ibid., 13.

appearance for he is totally unaware of any such event or even any such tendency. Few finally are those that place at the beginning of their books the warning that they have no notion of what might be meant by responsibility, that never in their lives did they have the experience of acting responsibly, and that least of all in composing the books they are offering the public.[28]

---

[28] Lonergan, *Method in Theology*, 16-17.

Chapter Three

"The Masterpiece"- *Method in Theology*

Be attentive! Be Intelligent! Be Reasonable! Be Responsible! Be in Love! These are the precepts that underline *Method in Theology* and the creation of the functional specialties.

<u>Method in Theology</u>

Lonergan's *Method in Theology* (1972) grows out of his previous accomplishment in *Insight*. It is a work, according to Charles C. Hefling, Jr., that "...is a lifetime's patient reflection on what theologians do, can do, and ought to do."[1] *Method in Theology* is described, along with *Insight*, by Frederick Crowe as Lonergan's *novum organon*.[2] What Crowe means by the term, *organon* comes from Greek antecedents, and, in his lectures on the importance of Lonergan's contribution, he builds on the importance of *organon* according to both Aristotle and Francis Bacon. Crowe describes *organon* in the following manner:

> At certain momentous points in history, the term "organon" has been used to designate an instrument of mind: not an

---

[1] Charles C. Hefling, Jr., introduction to *The Lonergan Enterprise*, by Frederick E. Crowe (USA: Cowley Publications, 1980), xiii.

[2] Frederick E. Crowe, "An Organon for our Time," in *The Lonergan Enterprise* (USA: Cowley Publication, 1980), 6.

instrument of the hand, like a hammer or nutmeg grater, or even so precious an instrument as a Stradivarius violin, but rather a developed talent of an incarnate subject a way of structuring our conscious activities, that has been of immense importance for the ongoing work of human race.[3]

Francis Bacon, develops the Aristotelian concept of *organon* further as "a new set of philosophical tools."[4] Above all, this novum organon is not just conceptual for Lonergan and has an absolutely practical role in the future of theology. Crowe writes:

There is a clue here, and more than a clue, to Lonergan's specific contribution to the intellectual enterprise, that enables us to recognize a fact quite central for assessing his thought and locating him in history. Namely, that whatever else his lifework may be, however penetrating his analyses and however impressive his ideas, his thought is ultimately oriented to the practical and is programmatic for the future. He has provided us with an instrument that is to be used, not just contemplated, and the real Lonergan of history is not so much the Lonergan studied and analyzed, discussed and debated, located and evaluated, but the Lonergan whose

---

[3] Ibid., 7.

[4] Whelan, *Redeeming History*, 9. Whelan notes that "…Lonergan more or less accepts the categorization of *Insight* and *Method in Theology* as a *novum organum* in an interview he gave, *Caring About Meaning: Patterns in the Life of Bernard Lonergan* (Montreal: Thomas More Institute, 1982), 119-120" (Ibid., 9 n.3).

achievement is still to be applied to the urgent tasks of the new age that we are facing.[5]

In the creation of an organon for the study of theology in his age, Crowe posits that "...Lonergan, like Bacon, has very clearly seen that the need of the times is not so much for a new set of answers to the problems of the day, as it is for a whole new beginning."[6] This was the work of a lifetime for Lonergan. Crowe writes in 1979: "So it was that for thirty-four years, from the start of his doctoral dissertation in 1938 till the publication of his *Method in Theology* in 1972, Lonergan labored to create an instrument that would do the job."[7]

Describing the monumental task that bringing *Method in Theology* to publication, Crowe states:

These bits of history are quite inadequate to convey the Herculean effort of thirty-four years that produced *Method in Theology*. To speak of going to the drafting-board three times at intervals of sixteen and eighteen years gives little idea of the courses, lectures, institutes, sets of notes and published materials that mark the stages of the struggle. But perhaps I have at least highlighted the fact that Lonergan's great work was indeed the end product of a lifetime of thought. It is on that work of a lifetime that his position in history will stand or fall.[8]

---

[5] Crowe, "An Organon for our Time," 6.
[6] Ibid., 14-15.
[7] Ibid., 15.
[8] Ibid., 23.

Part 1 of *Method in Theology*: Key Advances over *Insight*

Before an examination of the structure of *Method in Theology*, it might be wise to determine exactly to whom this text is addressed. Without a doubt, *Method in Theology* is not a beginner's guide to theology. Crowe states that "it is a book about those special tasks that fall to that special group within the church whom we classify as theologians."[9] Acknowledging the limited appeal of such a book for non-specialists in theology, Crowe explains: "To make the point by negation, *Method in Theology* is not a record of Christian living, or a manual of Christian piety, or a set of instructions on Christian doctrines and practise, or a book of poetry, songs, and praises celebrating the Christian experience. It is a specialized contribution and deals with theological specialization."[10]

The structure of the book itself is rather simple. Divided into two parts, Lonergan entitles Part 1 as "Background," and it consists of five chapters. Each of these chapters is devoted to questions of theological foundations, including "Method," "The Human Good," "Meaning," "Religion," and "Functional Specialties."[11] Part 2 is entitled "Foreground" and directly discusses each of Lonergan's eight functional specialties.

---

[9] Ibid.

[10] Ibid., 24.

[11] Whelan, *Redeeming History*, 143.

Functional Specialties

In order to grasp the concept of functional specialties, it is necessary to understand exactly how Lonergan came to the full realization of functional specialties. Frederick Crowe describes the year
1957 as a key moment in Lonergan's theological development. While
a professor of dogmatic theology at the Gregorian University, Lonergan, for his class on the Trinity, began to supplement his notes with
a section on theological method.[12] In his study on the development
of doctrine, Lonergan, aware of the oft-times "awkward" nature of
this analysis, begins to use modern historical research methods.[13]
Describing the situation in which Lonergan finds himself, Crowe
writes: "The fit is awkward…without full recognition of the role of
history as a factor prior to analysis."[14] The areas to which Lonergan
specifically applied historical research included both Christology
and Trinity, namely the developing understanding of the Person and
natures of Christ from Sacred Scripture and within Sacred Tradition
and the development of systematic theology in medieval scholasticism.[15]

---

[12] This is found present in Lonergan's notes and is titled "*Divinarum
personarum conceptionem analogicam evolvit* Bernardus Lonergan SJ." (See
Whelan, *Redeeming History*, 134 and Crowe, *Lonergan*, 86.

[13] Whelan, *Redeeming History*,134.

[14] Crowe, *Lonergan*, 84.

[15] Ibid., 87-88.

Using ideas coming to him from his study of Wilhelm Dilthey,[16] Lonergan makes a shift in his class presentation from the predominance of analysis and synthesis to a growing appreciation of the historical.[17] Coming from Dilthey's notion that one who interprets history has the desire to influence the present, Lonergan realized that, for the historian (and in his own thought), self-authenticity is essential.[18] Commenting on this aspect, Vernon Gregson notes:

What is true about seeking truth and value in general is also true about seeking truth and value in the area of religion, and, specifically to our point here, in the area of theology and in the work of theologians. Theologians are men and women who study in order to understand the origins and sources of

---

[16] Gerard Whelan notes the growing influence of Dilthey on Lonergan's methodological thinking. He states: "Like Dilthey, Lonergan's study of concrete historical developments begin to help him think more widely on questions of how what Crowe calls 'history as written' must be related to an interest in influencing ones (sic) own, current society, i.e., 'history as written about'" (Whelan, *Redeeming History*, 135 n.15).

[17] This shift in Lonergan's teaching in 1959 is apparent in his notes for his graduate class, *De intellectu et methodo*, which was later published as "Method in Catholic Theology," collected in Lonergan, *Philosophical and Theological Papers 1958-1964*, in *Collected Works of Bernard Lonergan 6*, eds. Robert C. Croken, Frederick E. Crowe, and Robert M. Doran (Toronto: University of Toronto Press, 1996): 29-53. See Whelan, *Redeeming History*, 135 and Crowe, *Lonergan*, 90-91.

[18] Whelan notes that, during this time period, Lonergan is also developing his concept of religious conversion, which fulfills his already established thought on intellectual conversion and moral conversion (See Whelan, *Redeeming History*, 136).

a religion and who try to communicate the meaning and significance of that religion to the culture in which they live, or to which they direct their concern...Theologians are, therefore, mediators between the riches of the past and the riches of the present. But that mediating must also be a discerning and an evaluating, for not everything in the past of a tradition is something to be treasured, sometimes far from it, nor is everything in the present culture something to be treasured, again sometimes far from it.[19]

No less than the individual interpreter does the community in which the interpreter lives has to be authentic. Gregson notes: "It is very difficult, if not close to impossible, to personally Be attentive, Be intelligent, Be reasonable, Be responsible, when the community that one is a part of consistently violates any or all of them...The achievement of truth and value, then, is not only a personal but a communal achievement."[20]

The Need for Functional Specialties

The need to have functional specialization is due to the fact that theology today is far too complex, too extensive, for one theologian to perform all the needed tasks well. Gregson notes:

---

[19] Vernon Gregson, "Theological Method and Theological Collaboration I," in *The Desires of the Human Heart: An Introduction to the Theology of Bernard Lonergan*, ed. Vernon Gregson (Mahwah, NY: Paulist Press, 1988), 74-75.

[20] Ibid., 74.

Each theologian does not necessarily engage in all the tasks, at least to any full extent, because the field of religion has become too extensive for any one person to do all the tasks well. Theology has become a collaborative endeavor...The eight tasks that Lonergan delineates for the theologian, then, are principles of collaboration among theologians.[21]

Lonergan, in *Method in Theology*, explains his idea of functional specialties by clarifying that it is not what is meant by modern academia's field and subject specialization. He uses Husserl's thought, describing field specialization as a way in which experts are constantly "dividing and subdividing the field of data" to be studied, and department and subject specialization as that which classifies "the results of [the] investigations."[22] Crowe defines field specialization as that "...which marks off an area by using a kind of material principle of division."[23]

Lonergan writes: "...functional specialization distinguishes and separates successive stages in the process from data to results."[24] In subject specialization, areas are delineated by a more formal principle. Crowe notes that: "This kind of specialization is more open in principle to some conceptual unity, though that very phrase suggests that any unity achieved would be rather abstract."[25] Crowe warns, however, "Besides, such a unifying principle is not apt to be widely

[21] Ibid., 75.
[22] Lonergan, *Method in Theology*, 125.
[23] Crowe, "An Organon for our Time," 24.
[24] Lonergan, *Method in Theology*, 126.
[25] Crowe, "An Organon for our Time," 24.

accepted. For it is in subject specialization, especially that the theological empires emerge, take shape, grow to power, and set forth on their imperial march to manifest destiny: hegemony over all lesser kingdoms."[26]

These two types of specialization are distinct in the fact that the former looks to the data collected and the latter looks to the results of that data. Breaking this distinction down further, Crowe explains Lonergan's third option: examining the process itself from the data result and from there, further distinguishing the functions which one moves from data to result. Noting that these functions are grounded in the dynamic operations of a consciously operating subject, one can then "anchor it [(the functions)] on firm ground and allow it to develop spontaneously from a naturally given base."[27]

With this in mind, Crowe notes that, for *Method in Theology*, "The focus is on the *functions* of theology, rather than divisions in the material object or the formal object."[28] There is a two-phase reality in this project for Lonergan: a mediated phase and a mediating phase. The mediated phase focuses on *retrieving* what past theologians have formulated within their own theological disciplines; the mediating phase is focused on *communicating* and *articulating* the data results from the past in a current cultural context. Thus, Lonergan's definition of theology is concretely manifested in these two phases of theology: "A theology mediates between a cultural matrix and the significance and role of a religion in that matrix."[29]

---

[26] Ibid.

[27] Ibid., 25.

[28] Ibid.

[29] Lonergan, *Method in Theology*, ix.

It is essential to realize that, with these distinctions, Lonergan is calling for a tremendous interdisciplinary effort. It is also essential to recall that the theologian is not a neutral observer in this effort. He or she must be an involved participant who bears the weight of a tremendous responsibility. Crowe articulates Lonergan's view of this responsibility by stating:

> This difference between the two phases is sharply accentuated in theology. I may indeed study "objectively" the religious past of my community, and do so with the same standards of science and scholarship that govern the neutral observers who work alongside me and investigate the same data. But I cannot stop there. A responsibility has been laid upon me which I may not shirk, a responsibility toward my own and later generations to hear sympathetically, to evaluate critically, to adapt intelligently, and to hand on conscientiously the heritage of my people. The difference is effected by my commitment as a believer; it results from my accepting, through conversion or the personal adherence which is the equivalent of a conversion, the beliefs of my community along with its ways and precepts and practices.[30]

---

[30] Crowe, "An Organon for our Time," 26.

Explanation of the Functional Specialties

Each of the two phases of theology has four, distinct functional specialties. This is related to the act that intentional consciousness has four distinct levels. Lonergan writes:

> The proper achievement and end of the first level, experiencing, is the apprehension of data; that of the second level, understanding, is insight into the apprehended data; that of the third level, judgment, is the acceptance or rejection of the hypotheses and theories put forward by understanding to account for the data; that of the fourth level, decision, the acknowledgment of values and the selection of the methods or other means that lead to their realization.[31]

Lonergan acknowledges that each of the first four functional specialties is analogous to a levels of consciousness. They are a specific implementation of each level of consciousness and build upon one another.[32] Describing the first phase of theology and relating each phase to a level of consciousness, Lonergan writes:

> In assimilating the past, first, there is research that uncovers and makes available the data, secondly, there is interpretation that understands their meaning, thirdly, there is history that judges and narrates what occurred and, fourthly, there is

---

[31] Lonergan, *Method in Theology*, 133.
[32] Gregson, "Theological Method and Collaboration: I," 75.

dialectic that endeavors to unravel the conflicts concerning values, facts, meanings, and experiences.[33]

Also in correspondence to each functional specialty is one of the four levels of conscious intentionality. Raymond Lafontaine analyzes Lonergan's schema in the following manner:

> ...the four levels of conscious and intentional opera-
> tions...which demand as their ethical imperative the fulfill-
> ment of the transcendental precepts...are enacted in the two
> phases of theological inquiries...yielding eight...functional
> specialties. The first four specialties reveal the religious situ-
> ation: they mediate an encounter with persons who have
> committed themselves within a religious tradition. Although
> they do not necessarily presuppose an explicit faith-stance on
> the part of the inquirer, the presence or absence of that foun-
> dational choice will have a major impact on the way of its
> tasks (of research, interpretation, history, and dialectic) are
> preformed. Inevitably, though, properly *theological* inquiry
> demands of the inquirer a foundational decision, which in-
> volves the choice to commit oneself (or not) within a partic-
> ular faith tradition.[34]

---

[33] Lonergan, *Method in Theology*, 134.

[34] Lafontaine, *The Development of a Moral Doctrine*, 46. Lafontaine brings up an interesting point, stating: "This decision, is identified as more immediately a *religious* rather than an intellectual-theological tradition" (Ibid.). He then quotes Lonergan to affirm this position: "In the first phase one begins from the data and moves through meanings and facts towards

Thus, one may say research (the first functional specialty) is related to experience (the first level of consciousness) and the precept: "Be attentive!"; interpretation (the second functional specialty) is related to understanding (the second level of consciousness) and the precept: "Be intelligent!"; history (the third functional specialty) is related to judging (the third level of consciousness) and the precept "Be reasonable!"; and dialectic (the fourth functional specialty) is related to deciding (the fourth level of consciousness) and the precept "Be responsible". These four tasks, as mentioned, ultimately are all about retrieving the data of the past. Gregson, in his interpretation, gives a masterful, practical application of this analogous relationship:

> The first four tasks principally concern the retrieval of the past: gathering ancient artifacts and texts (Research); discovering the meaning of what one has gathered (Interpretation); constructing a history of the time (History); and evaluating the significance of what one has arrived at in the first three levels (Dialectic). The relationship of these four operations to the levels of consciousness should be relatively clear. The goal of Research is data gathering or Experiencing. The goal of Interpretation is Understanding. The goal of History is arriving at what really happened in the past, which is an exercise in Judging. And the goal of Dialectic is considering the

personal encounter. In the second phase one begins from reflection on authentic conversion, employs it as the horizon within which doctrines are to be apprehended and an understanding of their content sought, and finally moves to a creative exploration of communications" (Lonergan, *Method in Theology*, 135-136).

significance of what the past has to offer and determining when there are conflicting views of the significance of the past, which is the most accurate and valuable; this is an exercise of Deciding. Although the goal of each of the specialties is one of the levels of consciousness, in fact, all of the levels are used in each specialty. For instance, the researcher must use his or her understanding, judgment, and decision to arrive at the goal of Research, establishing accurate data.[35]

Vernon Gregson gives a practical example of how these first four functional specialties are used in the study of theology. Using an example coming from biblical theology, Gregson explains:

A scholar might be interested in the original meaning of the passage in Matthew's Gospel in which the following words are attributed to Jesus: "I say to you that whoever divorces his wife, except for immorality, and marries another, commits adultery" (Mt 5:32). Research would involve establishing the accurate Greek text of a passage, and comparing it with other parallel passages in the New Testament. One would discover that Mark's Gospel does not make any exception for remarriage, even for immorality. Interpretation would involve understanding the meaning of the words during the first century A.D. and their use in Matthew's Gospel. Precisely what type of immorality justifies divorce? Is there a different standard for men and women implied in the passage-

---

[35] Gregson, "Theological Method and Collaboration: I," 75-76.

whoever divorces *his wife?* Can the wife initiate divorce? History would involve placing the statement attributed to Jesus in the context of the Jewish, Greek, and Roman views of the time which would further clarify its meaning. Is Jesus' statement going against the current of the time or is it in accord with other Jewish or Greek or Roman views? Does it continue a tradition or does it begin one? Dialectics would involve discerning the specific value or values the passages is seeking to affirm. How does the passage relate to the other teachings of the Gospel? Is the value of fidelity the point of the passage? Is Jesus seeking to raise the status of woman by limiting the reasons a man can divorce her? When the further question is asked, "Is this a teaching that has relevance only to Jesus' time or to the time of the writing of the Gospel, or to our own time as well?" one has moved on to the second four specialties.[36]

In the second phase of theology, each functional specialty is also analogous to a level of consciousness, albeit in reversed order. Foundations (the fifth functional specialty) corresponds to deciding (the fourth level of consciousness) and the precept: "Be responsible!"; doctrines (the sixth functional specialty) corresponds to judging (the third level of consciousness) and the precept: "Be reasonable!"; systematics (the seventh functional specialty) corresponds to understanding (the second level of consciousness) and the precept: "Be intelligent!"; and finally, communications (the eighth functional

---

[36] Ibid., 76.

specialty) corresponds to experience (the first level of consciousness) and the precept: "Be attentive!".

Vernon Gregson gives his interpretation of the second four functional specialties by stating:

> The second four specialties principally concern the present and the future. They involve reaping the fruits from the study of the past to create the present and the future. "Foundations" is articulating the change that has taken place in oneself or in one's community as a result of seriously confronting the values of the past. "Doctrines" is affirming the values one has discovered. "Systematics" is relating and integrating (making systematic) the values one is now affirming with one another and with the other values and meanings in one's life. "Communications" is passing on what one has arrived at, and what one values, to others.[37]

Gregson's practical application of the functional specialties to biblical theology can assist in coming to an understanding of the second phase of theology. He writes:

> ...Foundations would involve articulating the ground for the change in one's own attitude toward marriage and divorce, if it differed from what one discovered the Gospel to mean. And if it has not differed, Foundations would ground one's previous evaluation more deeply. Doctrines would involve

---

[37] Ibid., 77.

affirming the truth of one's new position. Systematics would be bringing this new truth into relationship with one's other positions and values. And Communications would be passing on, in as concrete and persuasive a manner as possible, one's new-found or renewed value.[38]

Lonergan himself offers a synthetic statement of explanation for his functional specialties. He states:

> ...experience, insights, judgments of fact, and judgments of value[:]...[(i)] So research is concerned to make the data available. [(ii)] Interpretation to determine their meaning. [(iii)] History to proceed from meaning to what was going forward. [(iv)] Dialectic to go to the roots of conflicting histories, interpretations, researches. [(v)] Foundations to distinguish positions from counter-positions. [(vi)] Doctrines to use foundations as a criterion for deciding between the alternatives offered by dialectic. [(vii)] Systematics to seek an understanding of the realities affirmed in doctrines.[39]

The Functional Specialties and the Task of Theology

These eight functional specialties are not separate and unrelated, but are in fact, intrinsically and functionally interdependent. In the estimation of Raymond Lafontaine, "This helps to preserve a

---

[38] Ibid., 77-78.
[39] Lonergan, *Method in Theology*, 349.

necessary *unity* to the theological task, which is often compromised by the endless divisions of field and subject specialization. It also helps to ground authentic theological collaboration; the unique contribution of each specialty is vitally important, if one is to grasp the full import of a theological question."[40]

The division of each of the tasks of theology into the functional specialties is key for four reasons. Lonergan articulates the reasons in the following fashion: first, it is more than a matter of simply saying that the matter is too broad and extensive for a single "professor" to teach. He states "...functional specialization is essentially not a distinction of specialists but a distinction of specialties."[41] It is done so as to "distinguish different tasks and to prevent them from being confused."[42] Lonergan further writes: "Different ends are pursued by employing different means, different means are used in different manners, different manners are ruled by different methodical precepts."[43]

Second, each of the eight tasks has eight different ends and thus, possesses eight different sets of methodological tasks to be distinguished. It allows the theologian to have clear and realistic goals for each step in his or her study. Third, Lonergan states "...the distinction and division are needed to curb one-sided totalitarian ambitions."[44] Each of the eight functional specialties is needed and each has its own "proper excellence." He reminds theologians that

---

[40] Lafontaine, *The Development of a Moral Doctrine*, 44-45.
[41] Lonergan, *Method in Theology*, 136.
[42] Ibid.
[43] Ibid., 136-137.
[44] Ibid., 137.

theology suffers when one of the functional specialties is neglected in favor of another, citing the Middle Ages as an example of this one-sidedness in theological studies.[45]

Fourth, the functional specialties are divided and distinguished so as to "resist excessive demands."[46] No one thinker, no one text, can address every single demand and answer every single question exhaustively.

Lonergan feels that the distinctions of the functional specialties can serve two purposes. The first, a major part, is "to produce the type of evidence proper to the specialty."[47] He gives the example of the biblical exegete doing exegesis; the historian doing historical research based on historical principles, and so on. The second, a minor part, is that each of the specialties is related to one another functionally. Lonergan writes:

> Especially until such time as a method in theology is generally recognized, it will serve to preclude misunderstanding, misinterpretation, and misrepresentation, if the specialist draws attention to the fact of specialization and gives some indication of his awareness of what is to be added to his statements in the light of the evidence available to other, distinct specialties.[48]

---

[45] Ibid.
[46] Ibid.
[47] Ibid.
[48] Ibid., 137-138.

As important as it is to understand the divisions implied in the functional specialties, it is also important to understand the unity and the fact that "none can stand without the other seven," and "(i)f all of the eight are needed for the complete process from data to results, still a serious contribution to one of the eight is as much as can be demanded of a single piece of work."[49] In order to establish a sure and certain base, each of the steps must be attended to and none can be bypassed.[50] Lafontaine puts it well when he states that "(T)he ultimate goal of the functional specialties is not to divide and conquer, but to celebrate unity in an interdependent diversity, for the sake of the coherent development of the Church's tradition and for the credibility of the Church's mission in the world..."[51]

Vernon Gregson points out that the eight functional specialties are basically answers to eight basic questions. For research, the

---

[49] Ibid., 137.

[50] Gregson, "Theological Method and Collaboration I," 77. Gregson continues, giving a practical example: "To build one's Foundations on what one would like the past to have been, or on what the past at first sight might seem to have been, is to build on a shaky foundation indeed. One of the reasons for the development of Scripture studies in the last hundred years is the recognition that a first reading of a text written almost two thousand years ago in a very different culture and in another language and with a community facing far-different problems is not going to reveal its meaning without careful and thorough study. The last four functional specialties depend on the first, therefore, for the integrity and richness. But the first four specialties are barren for the present and the future unless the further questions of the last four specialties are also attended to. *To know the past but not to bring its values into the future is a great waste of one's time and effort*" (emphasis mine)(Ibid).

[51] Lafontaine, *The Development of a Moral Doctrine*, 48.

question is "What are the relevant data?" For interpretation, "What is the meaning of the data?" For history, "What does it tell us (verify) about its time? For dialectic, "What value(s) does it reveal? For foundations, "Where do I stand with regard to its value(s)? For doctrines, "What will I affirm about its value(s)? For systematics, "How does this relate to my own or my community's other values?" For communications, "What and how will I communicate this to others?"[52]

The Challenge of the Functional Specialties for the Theologian

Lonergan is aware that he is not introducing a novelty into theology. Each functional specialty can, in some way, correspond to a more traditional aspect of theology. One might equate the first specialty, research, to textual criticism; the second, interpretation, to exegesis; the third, history, to Church history and historical theology; the fourth, dialectic, to apologetics; the fifth, foundations, to fundamental theology; the sixth, doctrines, to dogmatic theology; the seventh, systematics, to speculative theology; and the eight, communications, to pastoral theology.[53]

These functional specialties of Lonergan present a challenge to the theologian. It is a call that Lonergan first issued in *Insight*: "Knowing is not mere looking; it is a carefully experiencing, understanding and judging."[54] The true task for the theologian is not to simply retrieve the past theological tradition. He or she must then

---

[52] Gregson, "Theological Method and Collaboration I," 80.

[53] Lafontaine, *The Development of a Moral Doctrine*, 47.

[54] Gregson, "Theological Method and Collaboration I," 79.

also be certain to be open to using that data retrieved for present challenges and future possibilities. Gregson writes: "It is the error of stopping at History and not doing an evaluation of the significance of what one has discovered (Dialectics) and performing the other tasks necessary to bring the meanings and values of the past into the present and the future."[55]

Another challenge for the theologian is "to disregard the first five functional specialties and to begin with Doctrines and to pass on the Doctrines of the Church(es) from generation to generation without the challenge that comes from renewing again, in each generation of laity and clergy, direct contact with the original sources which gave rise to the Doctrines."[56] It should be noted that this is a particular challenge for those who serve as religious leaders within a particular community. In days before the discovery of contemporary critical investigative methods, this tendency was more common. "But in the present state of historical awareness, the attempt to pass on the tradition without the critical study of the originating texts of the traditions cannot help but give rise to the suspicion of defensiveness, or of laziness, or even of bad faith."[57] Lonergan writes:

> The medieval synthesis through the conflict of Church and State shattered into the several religions of the Reformation. The wars of religion provided the evidence that man has to live not by revelation but by reason. The disagreement of

---

[55] Ibid.
[56] Ibid.
[57] Ibid.

reason's representatives made it clear that, while each must follow the dictates of reason as he sees them, he also must practice the virtue of tolerance to the equally reasonable views and actions of others. The helplessness of tolerance to provide coherent solutions to social problems called forth the totalitarian who takes the narrow and complacent practicality of common sense and elevates it to the role of a complete and exclusive viewpoint.[58]

The theologian cannot be merely the mouthpiece of an established set of doctrines of a particular denomination of faith. The challenge is always present to broaden one's horizon, to go deeper, to ultimately move from the first theological specialty, Research, through all the functional specialties, to the final theological specialty, Communications, the end point of all evangelization.

Lonergan himself was very aware of this danger from the very start of his academic career. In his work, *Grace and Freedom* (1940), which served as his doctoral dissertation at the Gregorian University, Lonergan tries to live the Leonine adage, *vetera novis augere et perficere*. David Tracy, in his book, *The Achievement of Bernard Lonergan* (1970), describes Lonergan's intentions in this particular Thomistic study by stating "More exactly, it is his [(Lonergan's)] attempt to know precisely what the horizons of the 'vetera' were before attempting to transform them in the light of the expanded horizons of

---

[58] Lonergan, *Insight*, 256.

the 'nova.'"[59] Lonergan dives deep into the question of the very na-ture of grace, *gratia operans*, and in doing so, necessarily inserts him-self into the great debate between the primarily Jesuit-supported Molinists and the primarily Dominican-supported Banezians. In do-ing this study in historical theology, Lonergan launches into what he would later describe as his functional specialties, as well as keeping a clear eye on the importance of the dialectic of history, of moving from a classicist culture mindset and of looking at the concepts of progress, decline and redemption.

Lonergan, in his study of Aquinas, begins with his first two func-tional specialties, research and interpretation, in his desire to exam-ine this rather precise theological dilemma. However, perhaps what is more important for Lonergan is not so much an articulation of what exactly is the proper Thomistic interpretation of grace, as much as it is the arrival at a proper theological method to come to that un-derstanding. As impressive as Lonergan's achievement in the resolu-tion of the issue of freedom and grace (Patrick Byrne states: "Thus, Lonergan was able to achieve what neither the Banezians nor the Molinists could, and was able to resolve a 350-year-old dispute by employing historical methods."[60]) is, the fact that Lonergan deter-mines it is of the utmost importance to focus on Aquinas' cognitive theory to fully grasp Aquinas' theology of grace is even more impres-sive.

---

[59] David Tracy, *The Achievement of Bernard Lonergan* (New York: Herder and Herder, 1970), 22.

[60] Patrick Byrne, "The Fabric of Lonergan's Thought," *Lonergan Work-shop* 6, ed. Fred Lawrence (Atlanta, GA: Scholars Press, 1986), 25.

Lonergan writes in *Grace and Freedom*: "Unless a writer can assign a method that of itself tends to greater objectivity than those hitherto employed, his undertaking may well be regarded as superfluous," and further, "A historical study cannot but be inductive. An inductive conclusion, though it may be certain when negative, can for the most part be no more than probable when positive."[61] It is apparent that the themes for which Lonergan would develop in his later works, *Verbum*, *Insight*, and *Method in Theology* were very present in his doctoral dissertation.

In scholastic theology, "methodical questions were raised and methodological discoveries made, still their properly methodological aspect was not explicated."[62] Theology and theological method develops in historical circumstances- the Fathers of the Church were attempting to address individual theological questions that arose when the Church had the leisure (more or less) to actually ponder issues like the hypostatic union. The Scholastic doctors were trying to create a worldview to handle all possible theological questions. Manualism, in its conceptualistic manner, developed out of an over use of a deductive method, a "one size fits all" approach to theology. Therefore, in order to deal with this particular issue in the theology of grace, Lonergan studies what Aquinas actually wrote, rather than what others have written about what he wrote or what others have interpreted what he wrote. David Tracy writes: "For Aquinas at least was not interested in a theological science exclusively concerned with the end products of intellectual inquiry (concepts). On the

---

[61] Lonergan, *Grace and Freedom*, 155-156.
[62] Tracy, *The Achievement of Bernard Lonergan*, 37.

contrary, he embraced the theoretic attitude and scientific thrust pe-
culiar to the medieval period and employed the method implicit in
that period's achievements."[63] Aquinas moves from data to theory to
resolution of the theological question. Lonergan writes:

> There is a disinterestedness and an objectivity that comes
> only from aiming excessively high and far, that leaves one
> free to take each issue on its merits, to proceed by intrinsic
> analysis instead of piling up a debater's points, to seek no
> greater achievement that the inspiration of the moment war-
> rants, to wait with serenity for the coherence of truth itself to
> bring to light the underlying harmony of the manifold whose
> parts successively engage one's attention. Spontaneously such
> thought moves towards synthesis, not so much by any single
> master stroke as by an unnumbered succession of the adap-
> tations that spring continuously from intellectual vitality...[64]

Therefore, it is essential to understand the cognitive theory, which
ultimately informs the theological method used to investigate the issue of particular issue of the theology of grace, both in Aquinas and
in Lonergan.

Lonergan's functional specialty of research into the issue led him
to the second functional specialty of interpretation. In many ways,
Lonergan's approach to the questions of *Gratia operans*, moves from

---

[63] Ibid., 38.

[64] Lonergan, "Gratias Operans IV," *Theological Studies* 3 (1942): 573-
574, quoted in Ibid., 39.

each function specialty, in the sense that he is attempting to retrieve the past while simultaneously moving into the future. Ultimately, it is more essential for this study to retrieve a proper theological method before tackling the specific question itself. "(T)he content of speculative theology is the content of a pure form. It is not something by itself but the intelligible arrangement of something else. It is not systematic theology but the system in theology."[65]

Lafontaine writes: "Theology invites- indeed, it demands of the theologian- personal engagement, an explicit decision to 'take sides', to commit to a personal journey of faith, and (within Christian theology) to ecclesial belonging, to association with a specific religious tradition."[66]

Lonergan describes the decision of the theologian in the following manner:

It is a decision about whom and what you are for and, again, whom and what you are against. It is a decision illuminated by the manifold possibilities exhibited in dialectic. It is a fully conscious decision about one's horizon, one's outlook, one's world-view. It deliberately selects the frame-work, in which doctrines have their meaning, in which systematics reconciles, in which communications are effective.[67]

---

[65] Lonergan, 12 as quoted in Tracy, *The Achievement of Bernard Lonergan*, 42.

[66] Lafontaine, *The Development of a Moral Doctrine*, 49.

[67] Lonergan, *Method in Theology*, 268.

For the theologian, it is "not a set of propositions that a theologian utters, but a fundamental and momentous change in the human reality that a theologian is."[68] The theologian's objectivity comes from his authentic subjectivity and it entails a "total surrender to the demands of the human spirit: be attentive, be intelligent, be reasonable, be responsible, *be in love*" (emphasis mine).[69] It is precisely this aspect, of being in love, that is the role of the theologian. Theology comes out of religious experience and, from the reflection on that experience, the theologian's understanding, judgments, and decisions follow.[70] Pope Benedict XVI notes, "Knowing God is not enough. For a true encounter with him one must also love him. Knowledge must become love."[71] The functional specialties assist the theologian to articulate religious experience for himself or herself and for his or her ecclesial community.

Explanation of the Functional Specialties

At the very start of his explanation of the functional specialties, Lonergan clarifies that he is not speaking of hermeneutics. Stating that some have misused the phrase "hermeneutics," applying it to any and all aspects of the theological enterprise, he states that his

---

[68] Ibid., 270.

[69] Ibid., 269.

[70] Lafontaine, *The Development of a Moral Doctrine*, 49.

[71] Pope Benedict XVI visit to The Pontifical Gregorian University. http://priestlyformation.org/seminary-personnel/challenges-for-seminaries/.

functional specialties stand as a viable alternative for the theologian to secure his or her foundations.

Phase One: "Retrieving the Past"

Research: The First Functional Specialty

The first of the functional specialties is research. As previously mentioned, this functional specialty corresponds to the transcendental precept, "Be attentive!" Lonergan describes research in the following manner: "Research makes available the data relevant to theological investigation."[72] He divides research into two categories: general research and special research.

General research is the basis of this functional specialty, according to Lonergan. He states:

General research locates, excavates, and maps ancient cities. It fills museums and reproduces or copies inscriptions, symbols, pictures, statues. It deciphers unknown scripts and languages. It collects and catalogues manuscripts, and prepares critical editions of texts. It composes indices, tables, repertories, bibliographies, abstracts, bulletins, handbooks, dictionaries, encyclopedias. Some day, perhaps, it will give us a complete information-retrieval system.[73]

---

[72] Lonergan, *Method in Theology*, 127.
[73] Ibid.

On the other hand, special research is the implementation of general research. Special research pertains to the collection of data concerning a particular issue or concern, and, the more complete that the general research has been compiled and the more that the researcher is familiar with the data, the faster and easier it will be to accomplish the task at hand.

Lonergan later states that he truly regretted that he had not developed this first functional specialty further.[74] In fact, the chapter on research in *Method in Theology* runs only about three pages. The reason for the brevity, according to Lonergan, is due to the fact that "research is an enormously diversified category and doing research is much more a manner of practice than of theory."[75]

This practical functional specialty requires that the one who wishes to master such a skill needs to apprentice himself or herself to a genuine master in the field. Lonergan notes "one has to find out who and where there is a master that works in that further specialty on the basis of his research. To him one must go, join in his seminar, do a doctoral dissertation under his direction."[76]

Lonergan distinguishes between four different areas in which theological research is able to investigate. He lists them as human studies, religious studies, Christian studies, and Roman Catholic studies. All are "concerned with man,"[77] and each narrows its perspective more and more. For Lonergan, the main concern is how to deal with differing views among Christians in terms of relevant

---

[74] Crowe, *Lonergan*, 113.
[75] Lonergan, *Method in Theology*, 149.
[76] Ibid.
[77] Ibid., 150.

theological data. As to how one can deal with this variance of opinions in completing this functional specialty, Lonergan writes: "My answer is to let Christian theologians begin from where they already stand. Each will consider one or more areas relevant to theological research. Let him work there. He will find that the method is designed to take care of the matter."[78] He is fully aware that the theologian himself or herself needs to undergo both intellectual and moral conversion, and, if that has not yet occurred, then the functional specialties of dialectic and foundations will bring this to light and permit dialogue between honest theologians.[79]

Lonergan elucidates his thought in terms of the four levels of consciousness. He mentions that, even with research being on the experiential level, the researcher himself or herself is required to use all four levels of consciousness in order to complete his or her task. Lonergan gives a practical example, again using the field of biblical theology:

> So the textual critic will select the method (level of decision) that he feels will lead to the discovery (level of understanding) of what one may reasonably affirm (level of judgment) was written in the original text (level of experience). The textual critic, then, operates on all four levels, but his goal is the end proper to the first level, namely, to ascertain the data.[80]

---

[78] Ibid., 150.
[79] Ibid., 150-151.
[80] Ibid., 134.

Research is perhaps not the most glamorous of the functional specialties, but it is the one on which all of the others are based. Following the transcendental precept to be attentive, the research must also be intelligent, be reasonable, and be responsible so that all the work that follows is correct in articulating theology in today's cultural matrix.

Interpretation: The Second Functional Specialty

Building on the first functional specialty of research, interpretation is related to all of the other functional specialties yet is distinct from them. "The aim of interpretation is understanding the meaning of the data, often a text, which has been discovered in Research."[81] This functional specialty corresponds to the transcendental precept, "Be Intelligent!" When introducing the functional specialties, Lonergan describes interpretation by stating:

> While research makes available what was written, interpretation understands what was meant. It grasps that meaning in its proper historical context, in accord with its proper mode and level of thought and expression, in the light of the circumstances and intention of the writer. Its product is the commentary or monograph. It is an enterprise replete with pitfalls and today it is further complicated by the importation

---

[81] Gregson, "Theological Method and Theological Collaboration I," 82.

of the problems of cognitional theory, epistemology, and metaphysics.[82]

Lonergan reminds us of the vital place that interpretation holds as one of the functional specialties. In this section, he builds on the work that he had already done in *Insight* concerning the truth of an interpretation.[83] Like all methodologians, Lonergan begins by defining terms. He describes "hermeneutics" as principles of interpretation and "exegesis" as the application of these principles of interpretation to a given task.[84] It is clear that Lonergan is speaking of the written text, but he admits that his presentation on the subject can be applied to any of task in need of exegesis. Lonergan gives a stern warning to all those who might wish to overuse exegesis and apply hermeneutics to all texts. He states that "not every text stands in need of exegesis" and "the more a text is systematic in conception and execution, the less does it stand in need of any exegesis."[85] As a specific example of this, Lonergan mentions Euclid's *Elements* as a text that needs no interpretation. However, most texts, like that contained in

---

[82] Lonergan, *Method in Theology*, 127.

[83] Ibid., 153. See chapter 17 of *Insight*, "Metaphysics as Dialectic," 552-617. Lonergan himself makes the distinction between how he presents the truth of an interpretation in *Insight* and how it is discussed in *Method in Theology* by stating: "...observe how ideas presented there recur here in quite different functional specialties. For instance, what there is termed a universal viewpoint, here is realized by advocating a distinct functional specialty named dialectic" (Lonergan, *Method in Theology*, 153 n.1).

[84] Ibid.

[85] Ibid.

Sacred Scripture, being "narrative, descriptive, or symbolic" are in need of interpretation.[86]

Lonergan mentions the necessary distinction between a cognition mode of interpretation and a commonsense mode. The commonsense mode has no need for interpretation; this commonsense mode has perfectly understandable meanings, and there is no need for a detailed exegesis. There is a problem, however, when the text is readily understandable to a person of the time period when it was written, and with the passage of time, due to culture, language, and style, matters can become obscure. Lonergan states that there are three basic exegetical operations: first, understanding the text; second, judging how correct one's understanding of the text is; and third, stating what one judges to be the correct understanding of the text. Each of these exegetical operations will be explained in the following sections.

According to Lonergan, there are four facts that make interpretation very difficult. The sense of world consciousness and historical consciousness is the first of these dilemmas. The second is the growing understanding of the human sciences, "in which meaning is a fundamental category and, consequently, interpretation a fundamental task."[87] In the third place, faulty concepts of cognitive theory and epistemology make the task of interpretation difficult. Lonergan comments: "…interpretation is just a particular case of knowing, namely, knowing what is meant; it follows that confusion about

---

[86] Gregson, "Theological Method and Theological Collaboration I," 82.
[87] Lonergan, *Method in Theology*, 154.

knowing leads to confusion about interpreting."[88] The fourth problem in interpretation is due to modernity. Living in a post-Christian age, with a different philosophy and way of life, it is apparent that "the Scriptures have been removed from the context of Christian doctrinal development and restored to the pre-dogmatic context of the history of religions."[89] These problems in exegesis can only be addressed by the proper development and application of the theological method. Without this development, one cannot properly "distinguish and keep separate problems of hermeneutics and problems in history, dialectic, foundations, doctrines, systematics, and communications."[90]

In order to understand a text, Lonergan states that four component aspects are necessary. In the first place, the interpreter needs to understand exactly what it is that the author of the text is referring to. In his explanation of the component, Lonergan makes the distinction between a student of exegesis, who is learning about things he does not yet know, and a true exegete, who knows all the components already (the vocabulary, the history, the context, etc.), but who still has the task of exegesis to perform. The distinction made by Lonergan is not one of separation of roles, but actually of a distinction of emphasis. [91]

---

[88] Ibid.

[89] Ibid., 155.

[90] Ibid.

[91] Ibid., 156. Lonergan notes that the student of exegesis is also an interpreter. The student is working on basic knowledge, by and large. However, the exegete himself or herself has a deeper knowledge of language and

Lonergan rejects the "Principle of the Empty Head," by which he means that the less one knows about what an author is writing about, the better it is for the interpreter to come to a true meaning of a text, without imposing his or her own specific worldview on a text. This principle rests, according to Lonergan, on a "naïve intuitionism."[92] There is the danger of reading one's own particular view into the author's words, but the more one knows about the context, language, and history, the better for the development of a more accurate interpretation. An accurate interpretation of a text cannot take place unless one has gone through the steps of the levels of consciousness, of experience, understanding, and judging. "Knowledge is not just taking a good look," Lonergan had continually reminded his readers, and this is an example of that adage.

Second, in order to interpret a text, one needs to understand the words used in a text. Vernon Gregson, in his interpretation of this

---

culture, all of which is essential to understand and interpret the proper meaning of the text.

[92] Ibid., 157. On page 158, footnote 2, Lonergan quotes Bultmann to make his point: "Nothing is sillier than the requirement that an interpreter must silence his subjectivity, extinguish his individuality, if he is to attain objective knowledge. That requirement makes good sense only in so far as it is taken to mean that the interpreter has to silence his personal wishes with regard to the outcome of the interpretation… For the rest, unfortunately, the requirement overlooks the very essence of genuine understanding. Such understanding presupposes precisely the utmost liveliness of the understanding subject and the richest possible development of his individuality." From an article entitled "Das Problem der Hermeneutik," *Zschr. F. Theol. U. Kirche* 47 (1950), 64. Reprinted in *Glauben und Verstehen*, II, 230.

second component aspect, gives a practical application of the dilemma of misunderstanding the author's words. He writes:

> We have all had the experience in conversation of thinking someone was speaking about one thing and halfway through the conversation realizing the individual was speaking of something else. If that can happen in conversation in the present, it can even more readily happen in trying to understand the meaning of a text written centuries ago.[93]

The true interpreter, instead of concluding that the author of the text is incorrect, diligently analyzes the text again and again and even concedes that it might be he or she who is in error and not the author of the original text. This process, this exercise in intellectual integrity, continues until it is apparent that the author, not the interpreter, is the one in error. It is a shift that occurs from a preconceptual, commonsense understanding to a deeper understanding. Lonergan writes: "And this formulation itself is not to be confused with the judgments one makes on the truth of the understanding and formulation. One has to understand if one is to formulate what one has understood. One has to understand and formulate if one is to pass judgment in any explicit fashion."[94] Understanding is the key to what Lonergan describes as a hermeneutical circle: "The meaning of a text is an intentional entity."[95] The focus must be on the unity of the text,

---

[93] Gregson, "Theological Method and Theological Collaboration I," 83.
[94] Lonergan, *Method in Theology*, 159.
[95] Ibid.

and, at the same time, the unity can only be comprehended by what each of the parts reveals. "It is a self-correcting process of learning that spirals into the meaning of the whole by using each new part to fill out and qualify and correct the understanding reached in reading the earlier parts."[96] The rule of exegesis needs to be followed and followed thoroughly; however, "(u)nderstanding a text is, at its root, an exercise of the second level of consciousness, our capacity to arrive at the liberating and expanding joy of insight."[97]

Third, the interpreter needs to understand himself or herself in order to arrive at the proper meaning of a text. This is accomplished by growing in knowledge of the thought process and behavior of the people alive during the time that the text was written. While fully acknowledging that the way of acting and thinking of these ancient people is not his or her own experience, one can comprehend the culture and mindset of earlier people. It is an exercise in understanding another's "common sense." Lonergan warns, however:

> The phrase, understanding another's common sense, must not be misunderstood. It is not a matter of understanding what common sense is: that is the task of the cognitional theorist. It is not making another's common sense one's own, so that one would go about speaking and acting like a fifth-century Athenian or a first-century Christian. But, just as common sense itself is a matter of understanding what to say and what to do in any of a series of situations that commonly

---

[96] Ibid.
[97] Gregson, "Theological Method and Theological Collaboration I," 84.

arise, so understanding another's common sense is a matter of understanding what he would say and what he would do in any of the situations that commonly arose in his place and time.[98]

The fourth and final aspect of coming to understand a text involves understanding oneself. One can understand the great works of the past and present and allow these texts to challenge the interpreter himself or herself to grow. Lonergan calls this type of text a "classic."[99] Gregson comments:

The Scriptures, Plato, Aristotle, Shakespeare, the great novelists, etc., challenge us to alter our own view of ourselves and of our values, if we are to appreciate what they have to offer. They challenge us to a conversion, sometimes intellectual, sometimes moral, sometimes religious. We have all had the experience of picking up a book and not appreciating it or

---

[98] Lonergan, *Method in Theology*, 160-161.

[99] Ibid., 161. Lonergan uses Friedrich Schlegel's definition of classic: "A classic is a writing that is never fully understood. But those that are educated and educate themselves must always want to learn more from it." Lonergan takes this quote from H. G. Gadamer, *Wahrheit und Methode* (Tübingen: Mohr, 1960), 274 no. 2.

Here it should be noted that Lonergan's idea of a classic is similar to that of his student, David Tracy. Tracy defines a classic as "…those texts, events, images, persons, rituals and symbols which are assumed to disclose permanent possibilities of meaning and truth…" (David Tracy, *The Analogical Imagination: Christian Theology and the Culture of Pluralism*, (New York: Crossroad Publishing Company, 1981), 68).

seeing its point and then, months or years later, picking it up again and having it speak to our experience. The spatially separated marks on the page haven't changed, we have.[100]

It is also essential that the interpreter also know what others who have interpreted the text in the past have said. Each text comes with its own tradition behind it. It is a difficult task to come to know which of the past interpretations are correct. "It involves using all of one's personal resources, all of one's desire to know the truth. It calls for personal authenticity."[101] It also calls for the interpreter to have communal authenticity. The interpreter cannot merely focus on what his particular community wants to achieve in the interpretation of a text. There is no room for proof-texting. The interpreter needs to be able to judge not only the authenticity of the text, but also the authenticity of the tradition. Lonergan writes, recalling the concepts of personal and group bias: "So the unauthenticity of individuals becomes the unauthenticity of a tradition. Then, in the measure a subject takes the tradition, as it exists, for his standard, in that measure he can do no more than authentically realize unauthenticity."[102] Gregson comments: "Personal authenticity and communal authenticity are both the means and the goal of the functional specialties."[103]

In terms of judging one's own interpretation of something as correct, Lonergan refers us to the criterion established for

---

[100] Gregson, "Theological Method and Theological Collaboration I," 84.

[101] Ibid., 85.

[102] Lonergan, *Method in Theology*, 80.

[103] Gregson, "Theological Method and Theological Collaboration I," 85.

commonsense insights, which he detailed in *Insight*.[104] He reminds the readers that the interpreter begins not with the relevant questions, but with one's own *Fragestellung* (viewpoint interests). This, as mentioned before, can color one's own interpretation of the text.[105] The key insight comes to the interpreter, having set aside his or her own concerns and agenda, namely that his or her role is to communicate the thought and viewpoint of the author whom he or she is studying. The interpreter must know the context, which Lonergan defines as more than just in a simple, heuristic fashion. It is "the interweaving of questions and answers in limited groups…" and "a nest of interlocked or interwoven questions and answers."[106] After addressing this single topic, when all relevant questions are exhausted, then and only then can one possibly make a judgment. Knowing what questions are the correct ones to ask is also essential for the interpreter.

---

[104] Lonergan, *Insight*, 308-324. Lonergan summarizes this in *Method in Theology*: "The criterion is whether or not one's insights are invulnerable, whether or not they hit the bull's eye, whether or not they meet *all* relevant questions so that there are no further questions that can lead to further insights and so complement, qualify, correct the insights already possessed" (Lonergan, *Method in Theology*, 162).

[105] Lonergan, *Method in Theology*, 162-163. To elaborate on this point, Lonergan brings up his own personal experience. He writes: "My own experience of this change was in writing my doctoral dissertation. I had been brought up a Molinist. I was studying St. Thomas' Thought on *Gratia Operans*, a study later published in *Theological Studies*, 1941-1942. Within a month or so it was completely evident to me that Molinism had no contribution to make to an understanding of Aquinas" (Ibid., 163 no. 8).

[106] Ibid.

Finally, as to how one can correctly state the meaning of the text, Lonergan reminds us again of the role of the interpreter. True, he goes through experience, understanding, and judgment, but for a specific purpose, namely, "to understand, and the understanding he seeks is, not the understanding of objects, which pertains to the systematics of the second phase, but the understanding of texts, which pertains to the first phase of theology, to theology not as speaking to the present but as listening, as coming to listen to the past."[107]

Gregson sums up this functional specialty well when he writes: "In sum, one arrives at a correct interpretation of a text by answering all of the relevant questions that the text poses. And one gets to that point by using all of one's intellectual capacity, all of one's desire to know, and all that one has learned from others who have used their capacities before you."[108]

History: The Third Functional Specialty

Lonergan begins his explanation of the third functional specialty with his definition of history. He writes, "There is history (1) that is

---

[107] Ibid., 168. Lonergan reminds the reader of two things: first, that when one encounters a text, one is applying all of the functional specialties and that it is essential to remember that each of the functional specialties has eight distinct operations and eight interdependent but distinct ends; and second, that it is near impossible for one individual to apply all the functional specialties to a single text. This is why it is essential for specialists to collaborate with one another.

[108] Gregson, "Theological Method and Theological Collaboration I," 86.

written about, and there is history (2) that is written."[109] In his preface
to this chapter, Lonergan makes a bold statement:

> The precise object of historical inquiry and the precise nature
> of historical investigation are matters of not a little obscurity.
> This is not because there are no good historians. It is not be-
> cause good historians have not by and large learnt what to
> do. It is mainly because historical knowledge is an instance
> of knowledge, and few people are in possession of a satisfac-
> tory cognitional theory.[110]

Lonergan begins his study of the role of the historian by exploring
the difference between an exegete and a historian. The exegete's role
is to determine what is meant by meaningful speech and action. The
historian, however, is tasked with going beyond simply determining
what others have meant to truly grasp "what was going forward in
particular groups at particular places and times."[111] Lonergan states

---

[109] Lonergan, *Method in Theology*, 175.

[110] Ibid.

[111] Ibid., 178. Lonergan defines "going forward" as: "I mean to exclude
the mere repetition of a routine. I mean the change that originated the routine and its dissemination. I mean process and development but, no less,
decline and collapse" (Ibid., 178-179). With this statement, Lonergan ties
his view of history (progress-decline-redemption) with his view of the role
of the historian. He elaborates: "History, then, grows out of history. Critical
history was a leap forward from precritical history. Precritical history was
a leap forward from stories and legends. Inversely, the more history one
knows, the more data lie in one's purview, the more questions one can ask,
and the more intelligently one can ask them" (Ibid., 187).

that the historian's role is to see "how God disposed the matter, not by theological speculation, not by some world-historical dialectic, but through particular human agents."[112] The historian states what most people do not know. There are four reasons, according to Lonergan, for this ignorance on the part of most:

The first reason is that experience is individual, whereas historical data derives from collective experiences; second, history comes not only from the intended results but also from unintentional aspects; third, history is unpredictable, and one can only know the results of history after it has occurred; and fourth, history is more than just information gathering but instead involves analysis of all "interlocking discoveries that bring to light the significant issues and operative factors."[113]

For Lonergan, history is more than just experiencing but involves each aspect of the cognitive process: thus, the knower must have historical experience, historical understanding, and historical judging. Ultimately, the historian has to be the one to grasp the entire scope of events. This call to always go deeper, to not just remain content with superficial, surface knowledge, is consistent with Lonergan's cognitive theory. It is the threefold task of the historian to proceed "(1) from the data made available by research, (2) through imaginative reconstruction and cumulative questioning and answering, (3) towards related sets of limited contexts."[114]

---

[112] Ibid., 179.

[113] Ibid.

[114] Ibid., 184.

Lonergan makes a distinction between pre-critical and critical history in his attempt to come to a fuller comprehension of what had occurred in human history. By pre-critical history, Lonergan means stories created to foster a group identity or to create a devotion to a cause. This type of history is not meant to achieve knowledge of the truth but to create a type of unity among a people. There are five characteristics of pre-critical history. The first is that it is artistic, written in a creative, "catchy," and persuasive style; the second is that it is ethical, a tale of villains and heroes, establishing basic mores; the third is that it is explanatory, detailing why things are the way that they are; the fourth is that it is apologetic, in the sense of "correcting false or tendentious accounts of the people's past, and refuting the calumnies of neighboring peoples;"[115] and finally, it is prophetic, acknowledging that hindsight of the past can lead to preparations for the future.

Lonergan would place this pre-critical history not within the third functional specialty, but in fact, within the eighth functional specialty. In direct contrast, history must be critical; it must be done in detachment. A true historian cannot mix pre-critical and critical history; Lonergan states: "…it is attempting to serve two masters and usually suffers the evangelical consequences."[116]

Critical history has seven characteristics. Lonergan writes:

It is *heuristic*, for it brings to light the relevant data. It is *ecstatic*, for it leads the inquirer out of his original perspectives

---

[115] Ibid., 185.
[116] Ibid.

and into the perspectives proper to his object. It is *selective*, for out of a totality of data it selects those relevant to the understanding achieved. It is *critical*, for it removes form one use or context to another the data that might otherwise be thought relevant to present tasks. It is *constructive*, for the data that are selected are knotted together by the vast and intricate web of interconnecting links that cumulatively came to light as one's understanding progressed.[117]

The historian has to understand his sources, and having understood these sources, he or she then has to use these sources to understand the object to which they are relevant.[118] The historian is called to operate on the third level of consciousness so that he might judge what is true and what is false. He or she must be strongly aware of the danger of group and individual bias, of shaping history to one's own (or one's group's) needs. It is a call for the historian to go beyond relativism. Lonergan states, "It is a commonplace for theorists of history to struggle with the problems of historical relativism."[119] "…(R)elativism has lost hope about the attainment of truth."[120] It is a difficult

---

[117] Ibid., 188-189.

[118] Ibid., 189.

[119] Ibid., 195.

[120] Ibid., 217. Gregson comments on this point: "There is no question that objectivity with regard to history is difficult to attain. But to affirm a full relativist position, namely, in this instance, that one view of the past is as good as another, flies in the face of significant experience to the contrary. If relativism were correct, the most off-handed view of the past should deserve the same respect as the most careful and thoroughgoing study. And no one should bother to correct his or her own previous view on the basis

task for the historian to arrive at objectivity as much as he can in the very human field of history. History is not completely subjective, as relativists claim, nor is it completely objective. Unlike a science where one can back up one's hypotheses with experimentation, history involves human self-understanding. Nor is history a completely objective field, as in the case of a naïve realist. Gregson comments on this point:

> ...there are also views which would imply a facile objectivity in historical research. In these views, the work of historians would be to assemble the data of their historical research and let the results speak for themselves. These views too would appear to have some plausibility. For the data that historians assemble can, in principle, be examined and seen by all. But to take such a view is again to fall into the error of considering that knowing is like looking. If you can see it, you can understand it and know what it means. It is a scissors and paste view of history.[121]

In order to combat relativism, Lonergan posits the notion of perspectivism. He writes: "Where relativism has lost hope about the

---

of new evidence, since the second understanding has no more claim to being correct than the first. No one can live a complete relativist position, for no growth of knowledge would be possible. Even a relativist considers his position on relativism more correct than the position he opposes, or the position he held before" (Gregson, "Theological Method and Theological Collaboration I," 88-89).

[121] Ibid., 89.

attainment of truth, perspectivism stresses the complexity of what the historian is writing about."[122] One who grasps perspectivism understands that "not all elements of historical knowledge are equally subject to revision."[123]

Even historians become part of history itself, due to the fact that the historian, in his or her inability to come to complete objectivity, is very much part of his or her own time period, reflecting the perspective of that particular period. Gerard Whelan, commenting on this reality, notes: "…Lonergan suggest that while different historians may investigate the same historical reality, they will usually ask different questions of it. This is because the historian is a finite being and will inevitably be selective regarding what questions he or she finds interesting."[124] Lonergan himself comments:

> In brief, the historical process itself and, within it, the personal development of the historian give rise to a series of different standpoints. The different standpoints give rise to different selective processes. The different selective processes give rise to different histories that are (1) not contradictory,

---

[122] Lonergan, *Method in Theology*, 217.

[123] Gregson, "Theological Method and Theological Collaboration I," 90. Gregson elaborates on Lonergan's point by giving a practical example: "The motivations for Brutus' killing Caesar will likely never be all known, but it is quite improbable that later history will discover that it was not Brutus that killed Caesar, but rather that Caesar who killed Brutus! In other words, historical knowledge approaches certainty with regard to many events and situations, even if it only establishes probable correlations in other instances" (Ibid.).

[124] Whelan, *Redeeming History*, 146.

(2) not complete information and not complete explanation, but (3) incomplete and approximate portrayals of an enormously complex reality.[125]

Ultimately, the historian is called to have a shift in horizon. Lonergan employs the thought of Wilhelm Dilthey (1833-1911) in his creation of the functional specialties. Dilthey acknowledges that all historians are required to be surprised by what is discovered and learned. According to Dilthey, the historian must be a student of the principle of "life" (*Leben*). Lonergan comments on Dilthey by stating: "Dilthey's basic step may be conceived as a transposition of Hegelian thought from idealist *Geist* to human *Leben*. Hegel's objective spirit returns, but now it is just the integral of the objectification effected in concrete human living. Living expresses itself."[126]

Gerard Whelan comments:

By this he suggests that historians need, so to speak, to "get behind," the actions and statements of historical figures and to recognize the values of others is profoundly different from trying to study objects that do not have intelligence or freedom…He suggests that the good historian must have a firm grasp of the "worldview" (*Weltanschauung*) of the cultures of the past, and that he should recognize how these worldviews represent a value-system or basic horizon.[127]

---

[125] Lonergan, *Method in Theology*, 218-219.
[126] Ibid., 210.
[127] Whelan, *Redeeming History*, 115.

The historian eventually has to go, after experiencing, understanding, and judging, to the level of deciding. After the research has been completed, the interpretation accomplished, and the history determined, then one has to answer a key question: "What effect will I let this have on my life?" or "What will I do about what I know?"[128] The functional specialty that deals on the level of personal decision and choice is the fourth functional specialty: Dialectic.

The Fourth Functional Specialty: Dialectic

Vernon Gregson, in describing this functional specialty, writes:

Dialectic involves evaluation. But evaluation of what? An evaluation of differing accounts of the past or the present, an evaluation of the relative worth of different viewpoints. In short, an evaluation of the different movements and currents of human history....These are questions for evaluation. But who will evaluate? You and I. And on what grounds? On the grounds of what we already know and what we already value and on that "more" which our study of the lives of the great teachers (or saviors) challenges us to recognize and to value.[129]

---

[128] Vernon Gregson, "Theological Method and Theological Collaboration II," in *The Desires of the Human Heart: An Introduction to the Theology of Bernard Lonergan*, ed. Vernon Gregson (Mahwah, NY: Paulist Press, 1988), 92.

[129] Ibid., 93. It should be noted that Dialectic, the fourth functional specialty (and the end of the first phase) and Foundations, the fifth functional

Dialectic operates on the fourth level of consciousness. Primarily, it has two tasks, according to Lonergan: "It has to add to the history that grasps what was going forward a history that evaluates achievements, that discerns good and evil."[130] Its second task is to evaluate differences in the work of historians among themselves. Lonergan states: "dialectic...deals with conflicts."[131] Dialectic deals with differences; these differences go beyond what Lonergan calls "innocent differences" to what he refers to as "gross differences."[132] These differences are not caused by lack of perspective or lack of information.[133] These "gross differences" are caused by "explicit or implicit cognitional theory, an ethical stance, a religious outlook."[134] They can only be resolved with a change in horizon and genuine intellectual, moral, and spiritual conversion.

Lonergan begins his discussion on dialectic by stating what he means by "horizon." He states that "As fields of vision vary with one's standpoint, so too the scope of one's knowledge and the range of one's interests vary with the period in which one lives, one's social background and milieu, one's education and personal development."[135] Horizon is the structure, derived from one's experiences, desires, intentions, and limitations, to which one appeals when

---

specialty (and the beginning of the second phase) both operate on the level of personal decision, evaluation, and choice.

[130] Lonergan, *Method in Theology*, 246.

[131] Ibid., 235.

[132] Whelan, *Redeeming History*, 147-148.

[133] Lonergan, *Method in Theology*, 246.

[134] Ibid., 235.

[135] Ibid., 236.

setting goals or explaining one's deeds. Lonergan states: "Horizons then are the sweep of our interests and of our knowledge; they are the fertile source of further knowledge and care; but they also are the boundaries that limit our capacities for assimilating more than we already have attained."[136] A horizontal exercise of freedom can lead one to come to an "about-face" and have a new beginning: this is what Lonergan calls conversion and it is at the root of this fourth functional specialty, dialectics.

The concept of conversion as detailed in *Method in Theology* has its roots in *Insight*. Just as theological method was always a concern for Lonergan, even from his earliest days, Lonergan believed *Insight* and *Method in Theology* were two parts of a single thought: the absolute necessity to have a clear, concise theological method. William Mathews notes that the first explicit reference Lonergan makes to intellectual conversion derives from a class Lonergan offered in 1951. Concerning intellectual conversion, Lonergan writes:

In the direct mode of cognitional activity, we can experience cognitional structure but not know it. Initially we know by what we are but don't know what we are. Actually understanding cognitional structure involves a duplication in us of the structure. The same structure that knows objects in the world applies itself to itself. This is a point that is too important to be left implicit. [137]

---

[136] Ibid., 237.
[137] Mathews, *Lonergan's Quest*, 244.

Mathews describes the genealogy of intellectual conversion in Lonergan from Lonergan's early studies in philosophy, particularly J.A. Stewart's *Plato's Doctrine of Ideas* and his earlier study of theology, especially in his conclusion that "what exists is not known by intuition but by judgment."[138] It is this pure desire to know that drives the need to come to judgment. Concerning this time period in Lonergan's life, Mathews states:

> It is a difficult enough thing to identify and differentiate the elements of cognition, to identify and become familiar with the referent of the words 'spirit of inquiry', 'insight', 'judgment'; it is quite another to understand the law of their relations. How, precisely, are sensing, imagining, questioning, understanding, thinking, and judging related? Given the strangeness of our desire to know and related insights and thoughts, it is a question that we should not take for granted. We need to be puzzled by it and make it our own if we are to follow the movement of Lonergan's mind.[139]

Lonergan's mantra, "Knowledge is more than taking a good look," likewise is key to understanding his thought on this matter. Moving away from a Kantian notion, Lonergan formulates a concept that the pure desire to know intends the concrete universe of being and is a "notion of being." He states:

---

[138] Ibid., 254.
[139] Ibid., 242.

The notion of being is the notion of the concrete in the same manner as it is of the universe. It is of the universe because questions end only when there is nothing more to be asked. It is of the concrete, because until the concrete is reached, there remain further questions. Hence it is not the single judgment but the totality of correct judgments that equates with the concrete universe that is being.[140]

Knowledge comes from following an "upper context," a six-point moving viewpoint. Lonergan describes the six points in this way:

The upper context was...constituted (1) by the invariant structures of experiencing, inquiring, and reflecting, (2) by the consequent isomorphic structures of all there is to be known of the universe of proportionate being, (3) by the fuller invariant structure that adds reasonable choice and action to intelligent and reasonable knowing, (4) by the profounder structure of knowing and known to be reached by acknowledging the full significance of the detached, disinterested, unrestricted desire to know, and (5) by the structure of the process in which the existential situation sets human intelligence the problem of rising above its native resources and seeking the divine solution to man's incapacity for sustained development.[141]

[140] Lonergan, *Insight*, 387.
[141] Ibid., 754.

Intellectual Conversion

Lonergan defines intellectual conversion as "a radical clarification and, consequently, the elimination of an exceedingly stubborn
and misleading myth concerning reality, objectivity, and human
knowledge."[142] At the essence, it involves a shift in the way that one
perceives reality. Fully aware that "knowing is not looking," Lonergan believes that one comes to objectivity not by this naïve realism,
but that reality is "given in experience, organized and extrapolated in
understanding, posited in judging and belief."[143] It is the shift to a
world mediated by meaning, going beyond sense perception to the
external and internal individual and communal experience, which is
verified by the community.[144]

Lonergan describes this attitude of "knowing as looking" as a
myth with many consequences. Among them would be the philosophical positions of naïve realism, empiricism, and idealism. He
writes:

The naïve realist knows the world mediated by meaning but
thinks he knows it by looking. The empiricist restricts objective knowledge to sense experience; for him, understanding
and conceiving, judging and believing are merely subjective
activities. The idealist insists that human knowing always includes understanding as well as sense; but he retains the

---

[142] Lonergan, *Method in Theology*, 238.
[143] Ibid.
[144] Ibid.

empiricist's notion of reality, and so he thinks of the world mediated by meaning as not real but ideal. Only the critical realist can acknowledge the facts of human knowing and pronounce the world mediated by meaning to be the real world; and he can do so only inasmuch as he shows that the process of experiencing, understanding, and judging is a process of self-transcendence.[145]

Although each of these philosophical positions differs concerning various points and all come from different horizons, they all share the one thought that knowledge derives from looking. Breaking oneself away from this awareness requires a true self-authenticity, a knowledge of one's self, and a knowledge of one's cognitive structure. Lonergan describes it as such: "It is to acquire the mastery in one's own house that is to be had only when one knows precisely what one is doing when one is knowing. It is a conversion, a new beginning, a fresh start."[146]

This intellectual conversion is essential for the theologian who wishes to avoid a fundamentalism, a literalism, when it comes to his use of the first three functional specialties and his implementation of the second phase of functional specialties. With the awareness that comes from intellectual conversion, the theologian can avoid the pitfalls that lie before him or her should he or she try to prescind from

---

[145] Ibid., 238-239.
[146] Ibid., 239-240.

the basic criteria of evidence and of critical understanding.[147] Gregson describes this habit of the mind by stating:

> Lonergan's criterion of intellectual conversion is not meant to be some "new" criterion. Rather it is meant to be a reflective grasp of the natural and active criteria of our own minds. These criteria manifest themselves spontaneously as questions: "What is the evidence for what you say?" "Why do you understand it that way and no other?" "On what do you base your assurance that your understanding is true?"…"What is the quality of your evidence?" "Are you sure you have all the relevant data, or are you leaving something out?" "If so, what?" "Why must the evidence be understood in the way you are proposing, and not in some other way?" "Are you sure the evidence supports your hypothesis?"[148]

Lonergan states: "Intellectual conversion is to truth attained by cognitional self-transcendence."[149] This cognitional self-transcendence is essential if one wishes to truly engage in dialectic.

---

[147] Gregson, "Theological Method and Theological Collaboration II," 95.

[148] Ibid., 95-96.

[149] Lonergan, *Method in Theology*, 241.

Moral Conversion

As one progresses in dialectic, one becomes more aware of the need to make decisions and choices, "from satisfactions to values."[150] Using freedom to exercise one's self-authenticity, he or she opts "for the truly good, even for value against satisfaction when value and satisfaction conflict."[151] Moral conversion, at its essence, involves the rejection of the purely selfish, pain-avoidance, and pleasure-enhancing self-service to a maturity of self.

Lonergan wisely notes that moral conversion falls short of moral perfection. He states: "Deciding is one thing, doing is another."[152] True self-authenticity must take into account the reality of general and individual bias, as well as the situation in which the individual finds himself or herself. Lonergan urges the morally converted to continue to develop one's knowledge of "human reality and potentiality," as well as to grasp the elements of progress and decline.[153]

---

[150] Ibid., 240.

[151] Ibid.

[152] Ibid. Gregson, commenting on religious conversion, notes: "Economic materialism, scientific determinism, early Freudian *id* psychology, and many forms of behaviorism use as a basic criterion in their theories that human beings are at base sophisticated stimulus/response mechanisms. Such views attempt to reduce human beings to creatures responsive merely to pleasure and pain. These views can be appealing both because of their simplicity and because they can indeed explain much of our behavior, and surely much more than we are usually willing to admit. *But they cannot explain all* (emphasis mine)" (Gregson, "Theological Method and Theological Collaboration II," 96).

[153] Lonergan, *Method in Theology*, 240.

In many ways, one might view moral conversion as a triumph over selfishness in oneself and in society. It is a call to move from a limited horizon to a deeper one. Lonergan comments: "Moral conversion is to values apprehended, affirmed, and realized by a real self-transcendence."[154] T. S. Eliot, in his play, *Murder in the Cathedral*, writes: "The last temptation is the greatest treason: To do the right deed for the wrong reason."[155] The theologian who is truly morally converted is able to be responsible, to know what, and perhaps more importantly, why he or she does what he or she does. True moral conversion requires one to be open to criticism for self-growth, all in the service of coming to know the truth of the statements one makes and the grounds one uses for analysis. Moral conversion must be lived and "(m)oral conversion of its very essence is orientated toward action."[156]

Religious Conversion

Lonergan describes religious conversion simply as "being grasped by ultimate concern."[157] Religious conversion, then, means moving from a focus on one's own personal concerns to matters of ultimate meaning and value. It is a horizon shift from the things and values of this passing world to the things and values that perdure.

---

[154] Ibid., 241.

[155] T.S. Eliot, *Murder in the Cathedral* (New York: Harcourt, Brace and Company, 1936), 44.

[156] Gregson, "Theological Method and Theological Collaboration II," 97.

[157] Lonergan, *Method in Theology*, 240.

"Religious conversion is to a total being-in-love as the efficacious ground of all self-transcendence, whether in the pursuit of truth, or in the realization of human values, or in the orientation man adopts to the universe, its ground, and its goal."[158]

This religious conversion is described as "other-worldly falling in love," "[a] total and permanent self-surrender without conditions, qualifications, reservations."[159] It is viewed by Lonergan not as a single act but instead as a "dynamic state" and is demonstrated as "an under-tow of existential consciousness, as a fated acceptance of a vocation to holiness, as perhaps an increasing simplicity and passivity in prayer."[160]

Religious conversion differs from faith. Lonergan delineates the distinction into three stages: in the first stage, there is an individual's experience of supernatural, unconditional love; in the second stage, there is the decision of whether or not to return this love; and third and finally, there is the affirmative decision to respond to this other-worldly love and this is to become a "being-in-love." Lonergan speaks of this in rather personalistic terms:

---

[158] Ibid., 241.

[159] Ibid., 240.

[160] Ibid., 240-241. Here Lonergan makes the distinction in the Christian tradition between operative grace, which is religious conversion (described as "the replacement of the heart of stone by a heart of flesh, a replacement beyond the horizon of the heart of stone") and cooperative grace, which is the effects of religious conversion (described as "the effectiveness of conversion, the gradual movement towards a full and complete transformation of the whole of one's living and feeling, one's thoughts, words, deeds, and omissions") (Ibid., 241).

Faith is the knowledge born of religious love…Of it Pascal spoke when he remarked that the heart has reasons which reason does not know…This apprehension…may be objectified as a clouded revelation of absolute intelligence and intelligibility, absolute truth and reality, absolute goodness and holiness. With that objectification there recurs the question of God in a new form. For now it is primarily a question of decision. Will I love him in return, or will I refuse?[161]

This sense of "being-in-love" is a powerful experience of the transcendent. Tad Dunne explains this notion in the following manner:

If we decide to believe, then we can see that our lover is unlike any earthly lover. I might love you with all my heart, but you did not give me my love. This lover comes to us by giving us our power to love, and nobody on earth ever did that. With transcendent love, we can imagine ourselves caught in a great circle of love, beginning from the One who loves us, pouring this thirst and desire into our souls, and pouring from our souls towards absolutely all goodness, truth, beauty, and order-which is what this One is. Our love is Alpha and Omega, both the source and object of our loving.[162]

---

[161] Ibid., 115-116.

[162] Tad G. Dunne, *Lonergan and Spirituality: Towards a Spiritual Integration* (Chicago: Loyola University Press, 1985), 111.

Dunne makes a distinction between implicit and explicit religious conversion, in light of the definition of religious conversion as "the subordination of all conscious activity to transcendent love."[163] He states that one who does not analyze the source and origin of this transcendent love would be in a state of implicit religious conversion. The one who has an explicit religious conversion is able to recognize in personalistic terms, "a Thou, a Someone, a named and loved term of an orientation."[164] He states: "And for those knowingly in love, it makes an enormous difference in how they ponder life's mysteries; it gives them a Thou to talk with."[165]

Lonergan describes how, for the converted, the triad of "see, judge, act" reveals "the eros of the human spirit, its capacity and its desire for self-transcendence."[166] Religious conversion permits the existential subject to become a "subject in love, a subject held, grasped, possessed, owned through a total and so an other-worldly love."[167] From this perspective, everything changes for the subject. He or she now has a new basis to "see, judge, act" and a new impetus to promote progress and reverse decline. Religious conversion transcends the established ends of intellectual conversion (truth) and moral conversion (value). Lonergan explains religious loving as

---

[163] Ibid., 113.

[164] Ibid.

[165] Ibid., 113. Dunne uses this discussion to explain Lonergan's fifth "transcendental precept," "*Be in Love!*" He states that "love" in this precept implies the human experience of love, but in reality, is a call to recognize transcendent love. Dunne writes: "...it is this fifth precept, Be in love, that gives us the power to obey the other four" (Ibid., 115).

[166] Lonergan, *Method in Theology*, 242.

[167] Ibid.

"without conditions, qualifications, reservations…with all one's heart and all one's soul and all one's mind and all one's strength."[168]

Lonergan also explains the opposite of religious conversion: sinfulness. Making a distinction between sinfulness and moral evil, he describes it as "the privation of total loving…a radical dimension of lovelessness."[169] This can, according to Lonergan, be disguised as a failure to go deeper, one allowing oneself to live superficially and to escape into creature comforts. This superficial level of living cannot be sustained. It will ultimately lead to "the absence of fulfilment reveals itself in unrest, the absence of joy in the pursuit of fun, the absence of peace in disgust—a depressive disgust with oneself or a manic, hostile, even violent disgust with mankind."[170]

The Conversions and Sublation

Lonergan notes that, because all three conversions involve a self-transcendence, one can posit a theory of sublation.[171] Value,

---

[168] Ibid. Lonergan admits "(t)his lack of limitation, though it corresponds to the unrestricted character of human questioning" is indeed otherworldly in the sense that its fulfillment is "joy, peace, bliss" (Ibid.).

[169] Ibid., 242-243.

[170] Ibid., 243.

[171] Ibid., 241. Here, Lonergan indicates that his notion of sublation is more akin to that of Karl Rahner in *Hearers of the Word*, rather that of G. W. Hegel. Lonergan states that sublation means "what sublates goes beyond what is sublated, introduces something new and distinct, puts everything on a new basis, yet so far from interfering with the sublated or destroying it, on the contrary needs it, includes it, preserves all its proper features and

according to Lonergan, "is a transcendental notion. It is what is intended in questions for deliberation."[172] Lonergan describes a scale of values to which one responds in feelings. He writes:

> Not only do feelings respond to values. They do so in accord with some scale of preference. So we may distinguish vital, social, cultural, personal, and religious values in an ascending order. Vital values, such as health and strength, grace and vigor, normally are preferred to avoiding the work, privations, pains involved in acquiring, maintaining, restoring them. Social values, such as the good of order which conditions the vital values of the whole community, have to be preferred to the vital values of individual members of the community. Cultural values do not exist without the underpinning of vital and social values, but none the less they rank higher. Not on bread alone doth man live. Over and above mere living and operating, men have to find a meaning and value in their living and operating. It is the function of culture to discover, express, validate, criticize, correct, develop, improve such meaning and value. Personal value is the person in his self-transcendence, as loving and being loved, as

---

properties, and carries them forward to a fuller realization within a richer context" (Ibid., 241).

[172] Ibid., 34. Lonergan distinguishes between intentional feelings, which focus on an object as simple as "hunger, thirst, sexual discomfort," and as complex as feelings motivate someone to do the good, and nonintentional feelings that include "fatigue, irritability, bad humor [and] anxiety," all with no immediate cause (Ibid., 30).

originator of values in himself and in his milieu, as an inspiration and invitation to others to do likewise. Religious values, finally, are at the heart of the meaning and value of man's living and man's world.[173]

Each level of conversion sublates the other. For instance, moral conversion sublates intellectual conversion, and religious conversion sublates moral conversion; however, one should not think of a linear sequence—intellectual conversion, then moral conversion, and then finally religious. Lonergan points out the true nature of conversion by stating:

On the contrary, from a causal viewpoint, one would say that first there is God's gift of his love. Next, the eye of this love reveals values in their splendor, while the strength of this love brings about their realization, and that is moral conversion. Finally, among the values discerned by the eye of love is the value of believing the truths taught by the religious tradition,

---

[173] Ibid., 31-32. Here it should be noted that Lonergan also formulated the scale of value in another manner: "Vital values of health and strength; with the social values enshrined in family and custom, society and education, the state and the law, the economy and technology, the church or sect; with the cultural values of religion and art, language and literature, science, philosophy, history, theology; with the achieved personal value of one dedicated to realizing values in himself and promoting their realization in others" (Lonergan, "The Response of the Jesuit as Priest and Apostle in the Modern World," in *A Second Collection: Papers by Bernard J. F. Lonergan, S.J.*, eds. W. F. J. Ryan and B. J. Tyrell (Philadelphia: The Westminster Press, 1975), 168-169).

and in such tradition and belief are the seeds of intellectual conversion. For the word, spoken and heard, proceeds from and penetrates to all four levels of intentional consciousness. *Its content is not just a content of experience but a content of experience and understanding and judging and deciding. The analogy of sight yields the cognitional myth. But fidelity to the word engages the whole man* (emphasis mine).[174]

The opposite of conversion is breakdown. Due to a lack of true self-transcendence, due to superficiality and a lack of self-authenticity, the progress made by individuals and cultures can quickly decline. Lonergan states: "Cognitional self-transcendence is neither an easy notion to grasp nor a readily accessible datum of consciousness to be verified."[175] However, even though it is difficult, it is necessary if one wishes to grow. Intellectual, moral, and religious conversions are the cornerstones of the fourth functional specialty, dialectic.

Lonergan describes the two levels of dialectic: the upper level, consisting of operators, and the lower level, involving the things that are operated on. He describes the upper level (operator) as having two main precepts. The first of these precepts is to develop a position, which Lonergan defines as "statements compatible with intellectual, moral, and religious conversion."[176] The second of these precepts is

---

[174] Lonergan, *Method in Theology*, 243.
[175] Ibid.
[176] Ibid., 249.

to reverse counter-positions, described by Lonergan as "statements incompatible with intellectual, or moral, or religious conversion."[177]

In order to grasp the concept of dialectic, one needs to understand that the first three functional specialties are deficient in two ways: first, history is concerned with telling what exactly happened. Operating on the third level of intentional consciousness, it does not concern itself with values, which would be an operation of the fourth level of consciousness. Second, interpretation is based not on an evaluative hermeneutics, which also operates on the fourth level of consciousness.

Dialectic's tasks, then, are to add an evaluative aspect to the first three functional specialties. The theologian engaging in dialectic is to be the one aware of "gross differences" that may exist in history or texts. He or she is to become more aware that the individual authors may not have arrived at the same level of conversion and are operating at different levels of differentiation of consciousness. Dialectic is

---

[177] Ibid. Lonergan notes that, prior to being "operated on," the material in question has to be "assembled, completed, compared, reduced, classified, [and] selected" (Ibid.). He defines each of these terms: "*Assembly* includes the researches performed, the interpretations proposed, the histories written, and the events, statements, movements to which they refer. *Completion* adds evaluative interpretation and evaluative history.…*Comparison* examines the completed assembly to seek out affinities and oppositions. *Reduction* finds the same affinity and the same opposition manifested in a number of different manners; from the many manifestations it moves to the underlying root. *Classification* determines which of these sources of affinity or opposition result from dialectically opposed horizons and which have other grounds. *Selection*…picks out the affinities and oppositions grounded in dialectically opposed horizons and dismisses other affinities and oppositions" (Ibid., 249-250).

difficult work for the theologian. It involves a radical call to self-authenticity that can only come from an ongoing effort. It involves a realism about oneself, about others, and about the world. Lonergan writes:

> Human authenticity is not some pure quality, some serene freedom from all oversights, all misunderstanding, all mistakes, all sins. Rather it consists in a withdrawal from unauthenticity, and the withdrawal is never a permanent achievement. It is ever precarious, ever to be achieved afresh, ever in great part a matter of uncovering still more oversights, acknowledging still further failures to understand, correcting still more mistakes, repenting more and more deeply hidden sins. Human development, in brief, is largely through the resolution of conflicts and, within the realm of intentional consciousness, the basic conflicts are defined by the opposition of positions and counter-positions.[178]

Above all else when it comes to the fourth functional specialty, Lonergan reminds us that among the four realms of meaning (common sense, theory, interiority, and transcendence), the one he has described the least as a differentiated realm is transcendence. He describes the gift of God's love as "spontaneously reveals itself in love, joy, peace, patience, kindness, goodness, fidelity, gentleness, and self-

---

[178] Ibid., 252.

control."[179] The theologian, in order to do his or her task, must deal with the dialectic that has plagued modern humanity—common sense and transcendence. Lonergan writes:

> Quite distinct from these objectifications of the gift of God's love in the realms of common sense and of theory and from the realm of interiority, is the emergence of the gift as itself a differentiated realm. It is this emergence that is cultivated by a life of prayer and self-denial and, when it occurs, it has the twofold effect, first, of withdrawing the subject from the realm of common sense, theory, and other interiority into a "cloud of unknowing" and then of intensifying, purifying, clarifying, the objectifications referring to the transcendent whether in the realm of common sense, or of theory, or of other interiority.[180]

---

[179] Ibid., 266. Here Lonergan makes the point that in "undifferentiated consciousness," God's love is expressed in reference to sacred places, sacred objects, sacred liturgy, and sacred offices. In differentiated consciousness, "When these three realms of common sense, theory, and interiority are differentiated, the self-appropriation of the subject leads not only to the objectification of experiencing, understanding, judging, and deciding, but also of religious experience" (Ibid.).

[180] Ibid.

The Fifth Functional Specialty: Foundations

This fifth functional specialty corresponds the transcendental precept: "Be responsible!" In bringing his reader to the second phase of theology, a mediated phase, where

> It was no longer to be content to narrate what others pro-
> posed, believed, did. It has to pronounce which doctrines
> were true, how they could be reconciled with one another
> and with the conclusions of science, philosophy, history, and
> how they could be communicated appropriately to the mem-
> bers of each class in every culture.[181]

It is in this mediated phase that a personal stance must enter into theological reflection. The sixth functional specialty, foundations, seeks to lay the foundations for the remaining functional specialties of doctrines, systematics, and communications. Foundations takes the work accomplished in the theologian in his or her personal con- versions and differentiation of consciousness and then "move[s] from the indirect discourse that sets forth the convictions and opin- ions of others to the direct discourse that states what is so."[182]

Vernon Gregson explains "Dialectic and Foundations then are really names for two poles of the same process. Dialectic is the name of the pole which is the content of our evaluations, and Foundations is the name of the pole which is who we have become through the

---

[181] Ibid., 267.
[182] Ibid.

process of making those evaluations."[183] Lonergan states that this fifth functional specialty of foundations differs from traditional fundamental theology in two manners: first, he indicates that "old fundamental theology" did not follow the first four specialties; and second, fundamental theology previously had been presented as a set of doctrines.[184]

Lonergan explains that at the basis of this functional specialty is foundational reality. He explains that this foundational reality is conversion.[185] Prior to this point, one could still perform the first four functional specialties as part of this mediating phase; one does not

---

[183] Gregson, "Theological Method and Theological Collaboration II," 101.

[184] Lonergan, *Method in Theology*, 131. By the phrase "old fundamental theology," it must be noted that Lonergan is referring to a pre-Vatican II concept of fundamental theology being solely apologetics. Gerald O'Collins, in *Retrieving Fundamental Theology: The Three Styles of Contemporary Theology* (London: Geoffrey Chapman, 1993), 40, describes contemporary fundamental theology as "that discipline which in the light of faith reflects critically on the foundations of theology and basic theological issues." In his (and Edward C. Farrugia's) *Concise Dictionary of Theology*, Revised and Expanded Edition (Mahwah, NJ: Paulist, 2000), 94, O'Collins defines fundamental theology as "That branch of Western theology which studies foundational issues: the divine revelation in the history of Israel and Jesus Christ; the conditions that open human beings up to this self-communication of God; the signs that make faith in and through Jesus Christ a reasonable option; the transmission (through the church's tradition and the inspired scriptures) of the experience of God's self-communication."

[185] Ibid., 267. Lonergan attributes the fruit of each conversion by stating: "...intellectual conversion as the fruit of both religious and moral conversion...moral conversion as the fruit of religious conversion...religious conversion as the fruit of God's gift of his grace" (Ibid., 267-268).

have to be implicitly converted, although conversion is present and operative in this first phase. It is here that the theologian must take the data researched and interpreted and then, take a side that he has consciously made concerning that data. By making these choices, "we not only determine the matters at hand we also establish our own character."[186] Lonergan writes:

> ...foundations occurs on the fourth level of human con-sciousness, on the level of deliberation, evaluation, decision. It is a decision about whom and what you are for and, again, whom and what you are against. It is a decision illuminated by the manifold possibilities exhibited in dialectics. It is a fully conscious decision about one's horizon, one's outlook, one's world-view.[187]

One becomes who one is by the decisions one makes. Lonergan re-minds his readers that this decision is "anything but arbitrary."[188] It is a personal journey from inauthenticity to authenticity and a "total surrender to the demands of the human spirit: be attentive, be intel-ligent, be reasonable, be responsible, be in love."[189] It is a triumph of awareness over unawareness; it is the work of a "good conscience."[190]

---

[186] Gregson, "Theological Method and Theological Collaboration II," 100.

[187] Lonergan, *Method in Theology*, 268.

[188] Ibid.

[189] Ibid.

[190] Ibid., 269. Lonergan states that "deliberate decision about one's hori-zon is high achievement" (Ibid.).

This "high achievement," although personal, is not a private affair. Lonergan notes that it is only within religious tradition that true development can occur. This, too, is a high achievement because "(T)o know that conversion is religious, moral, and intellectual, to discern between authentic and unauthentic conversion, to recognize the difference in their fruits…all call for a high seriousness and a mature wisdom that a social group does not easily attain or maintain."[191]

This change in personal horizon requires that the authentically converted person be willing to examine his or her own religious tradition to determine true and authentic value in that tradition. Authenticity of the group or the religious tradition is measured in the amount of service that it performs on behalf of humanity.[192]

Lonergan states that there are two ways in which one might think about foundations. The first presumes foundations as a "set of premisses (sic), of logically first propositions;" the second presumes a more complex manner, positing foundations as what is first in any ordered set.[193] The way one thinks about foundations has a tremendous effect on how one does theology. If one conceives of theology as propositional, one holds that "One must believe and accept whatever the bible or the true church or both believe and accept."[194] On the other hand, one might conceive of theology as "an ongoing,

---

[191] Ibid.

[192] Ibid. Lonergan warns the reader, "But how the group is constituted, who was the founder to whom it bears witness, what are the services it renders to mankind, these are questions not for the fifth functional specialty, foundations, but for the sixth, doctrines" (Ibid.).

[193] Ibid.

[194] Ibid., 270.

developing process," one that is not "static, deductivist," but one that "aims at decreasing darkness and increasing light and keeps adding discovery to discovery."[195]

For the theologian who has undergone a threefold conversion, it is a "fundamental and momentous change in the human reality that a theologian is."[196] Embracing this inductive style, the theologian recognizes that the language necessary to express religious living must be integrated into the lived cultural experience of the era. The theologian who truly has embraced a differentiated consciousness is able to move from common sense language and ordinary language to a new horizon of religious expression "only…limited by the extent of our conversions and the extent of our literary, artistic, and scholarly gifts."[197] The theologian must express his or her own faith from a perspective of interiority, relating who he or she is as a person of faith to other aspects of his or her life.

Lonergan describes religious experience as "decisional openness." Gregson explains this concept as "awareness, i.e., experience or consciousness, of our decisional openness to the Transcendent."[198] Operating on the fourth level of consciousness, the level of value, this religious consciousness is a response to transcendent value. The lived response to transcendent value is given in ethics, which is "value responded to [in]…the world of finite value."[199]

---

[195] Ibid.

[196] Ibid.

[197] Gregson, "Theological Method and Theological Collaboration II," 103.

[198] Ibid., 104.

[199] Ibid., 105.

Gregson describes Lonergan's concept of foundational theology as "reflection upon ourselves as experiencing religiously, i.e., as experiencing our decisional responsiveness to the divine."[200] Those who are operating on the level of religious value are different, not in the process of knowing, but in what they choose to attend to and in the manner they choose to do with what they know and believe.[201] He adds:

> The difference for the genuinely religious person is not in the process of knowing, but in the motivation for knowing and in the freedom for knowing. For if we really experience ourselves as being gifted, graced, by the divine, we can begin to let go of our neurotic, egoistic, group, and common sense biases. These biases are ultimately based on our fear that we will be hurt, or further hurt, and so we narrow our focus to what is for "me," or for "us," or for "now." Knowledge, which does not have "us" at the center, simply is not relevant. For a genuinely religious person, however, all knowledge about the real world is significant, whether it impacts me directly or not.[202]

Lonergan then details the theological categories necessary to communicate religious truth to contemporary culture. He makes a distinction between general categories, which are purely in the

---

[200] Ibid.
[201] Ibid.
[202] Ibid.

philosophical realm, and special categories, based on religious faith.[203] Working out of categories he had previously employed in *Insight*, with a primary thought being "A universe in which both classical and statistical laws are verified will be characterized by a process of emergent probability. Authenticity can be shown to generate progress, unauthenticity to bring about decline."[204] Lonergan notes that the method to be employed is transcendental and transcultural, in the sense that the realities of the formulation are not products of culture but instead produce culture.

General categories regard the objects not only in the realm of theology, but also in other academic disciplines.[205] Lonergan describes the base of general theological categories as "the attending, inquiring, reflecting, deliberating subject along with the operations that result from attending, inquiring, reflecting, deliberating and

[203] Lonergan, *Method in Theology*, 282. He notes that the distinction between general and special theological categories is not to be made by the methodologist (whose role is three-fold: "indicating what qualities are desirable in theological categories, what measure of validity is to be demanded of them, and how categories with the desired qualities and validity are to be obtained."), but by the theologian himself or herself engaged in foundational work (Ibid.).

[204] Ibid., 288. By "emergent probabilities," Lonergan basically describes the following: "For the actual functioning of earlier schemes in the series fulfils the conditions for the possibility of the functioning of later schemes…But what is probable, sooner or later occurs. When it occurs, a probability of emergence is replaced by a probability of survival; and as long as the scheme survives, it is in its turn fulfilling conditions for the possibility of still later schemes in the series" (Lonergan, *Insight*, 145).

[205] Lonergan, *Method in Theology*, 282.

with the structure within which the operations occur."[206] The subject here is the individual theologian and this process must happen also in the theologian himself or herself.[207] This process also occurs in the social group, not only in the individual. In a nine-fold distinction, Lonergan differentiates the "basic nest of terms and relations,"[208] and, from this broad base, "one can go on to a developed account of the human good, values, beliefs, to the carriers, elements, functions, realms, and stages of meaning, to the question of God, of religious experience, its expressions, its dialectical development."[209]

Special theological categories, on the other hand, concern theological topics exclusively. In order to understand this concept, Lonergan states that the categories must be explained in terms of methodological theology. Beginning with intentionality analysis and the transcendental method, he reminds us of the self-transcendent

---

[206] Ibid., 285-286.

[207] Ibid., 286. Lonergan further describes "nests and relations," which derive from the base of the general theological categories. He writes: "Similarly, the relevant attending, inquiring, reflecting, deliberating are the attending, inquiring, reflecting, deliberating that he has found to go on in himself; the consequent operations are the operations he has uncovered and identified in his own operating; and the structure within which the operations occur is the pattern of dynamic relations which, as he knows from his own experience, lead from one operation to the next. Finally, the subject is self-transcending. His operations reveal objects: single operations reveal partial objects; a structured compound of operations reveals compounded objects; and as the subject by his operations is conscious of himself operating, he too is revealed though not as object but as subject" (Ibid.).

[208] Ibid. This nine-fold differentiation can be found on pages 286-287.

[209] Ibid., 287.

nature of the human being. In terms of the intellectual, self-transcendence comes from growth in knowledge; for the moral, self-transcendence comes from pursuing and doing what is good. For the self-transcendent, affectivity comes from love. Lonergan writes:

> ...he was self-transcendent affectively when he fell in love, when the isolation of the individual was broken and he spontaneously functioned not just for himself but for others as well. Further we distinguished different kinds of love: the love of intimacy, of husband and wife, of parents and children; the love of mankind devoted to the pursuit of human welfare locally or nationally or globally; and the love that was other-worldly because it admitted no conditions or qualifications or restrictions or reservations.[210]

Lonergan gives examples of five sets of categories for foundations as a theological specialty. The first is gleaned from religious experience and focuses on the necessity for spiritual growth in the theologian himself or herself so that he or she can dialogue with others in a relevant manner. The second progresses from the individual to the group and "their togetherness in community, service, and witness, the history of the salvation that is rooted in a being-in-love, and the function of this history in promoting the kingdom of God amongst men."[211] The third set of special categories involves the movement in love from the individual to the community to the source of love,

---

[210] Ibid., 289.
[211] Ibid., 291.

namely God. The fourth set, Lonergan notes, derives from differentiation and is the transcendental base for dialectic. It involves examining one's own notion of Christianity to determine authenticity or inauthenticity.

Describing the fifth set, Lonergan writes:

A fifth set of categories regards progress, decline, and redemption. As human authenticity promotes progress, and human unauthenticity generates decline, so Christian authenticity—which is a love of others that does not shrink from self-sacrifice and suffering—is the sovereign means for overcoming evil. Christians bring about the kingdom of God in the world not only by doing good but also by overcoming evil with good (Rom. 12, 21). Not only is there the progress of mankind but also there is development and progress within Christianity itself; and as there is development, so too there is decline; and as there is decline, there also is the problem of undoing it, of overcoming evil with good not only in the world but also in the church.[212]

These categories are to be used to come to true authenticity. The base for general categories, according to Lonergan, is the human being, be he or she "attentive or inattentive, intelligent or slow-witted, reasonable or silly, responsible or irresponsible."[213] He notes that for the special theological categories, the base shifts from the human to the

---

[212] Ibid.
[213] Ibid., 292.

Christian, forcing the individual to ask himself or herself about the genuineness of his or her love of God and neighbor.

Above all else, this fifth functional specialty invites the theologian to put into practice his or her self-authenticity, to be a "Christian subject effecting self-appropriation and employing this heightened consciousness both as a basis for methodical control in doing theology and, as well, as an *a priori* whence he can understand other men, their social relations, their history, their religion, their rituals, their destiny."[214] Foundation's main concern is highlighting how he upward movement of our own self-transcendence is crowned and embraced by the transforming downward movement of God's gift. The true foundation is the experience of the love that is God. Lonergan writes:

> It is as though a room were filled with music though one can have no sure knowledge of its source. There is in the world, as it were, a charged field of love and meaning; here and there it reaches a notable intensity; but it is ever unobtrusive, hidden, inviting each of us to join. And join we must if we are to perceive it, for our perceiving is through our own loving.[215]

---

[214] Ibid.

[215] Ibid., 290. It should be noted that in this passage Lonergan is speaking about the experience of Olivier Rabut (1911-1991) in his book, *L'expérience religieuse fondamentale* (Tournai: Castermann, 1969), 168.

The Sixth Functional Specialty: Doctrines

The sixth functional specialty, doctrines, corresponds to the transcendental precept, "Be Reasonable!" He defines this functional specialty by stating:

> Doctrines express judgments of fact and judgments of value. They are concerned, then, with the affirmations and negations not only of dogmatic theology but also of moral, ascetical, mystical, pastoral, and any similar branch. Such doctrines stand within the horizon of foundations. They have their precise definition from dialectic, their positive wealth of clarification and development from history, their grounds in the interpretation of the data proper to theology.[216]

At the very start of his discussions on doctrines, Lonergan clearly distinguishes among types of doctrine. He divides them into "primary sources, church doctrines, theological doctrines, methodological doctrine, and the application of a methodological doctrine that results in a functional specialty named doctrines."[217] In describing primary sources, Lonergan further distinguishes between "the doctrine of the original message" and "doctrines about this doctrine."[218] Following primary sources is what Lonergan calls "church doctrines," namely doctrines that derive from the New Testament and

---

[216] Ibid., 132.
[217] Ibid., 295.
[218] Ibid.

early Church decisions. He notes that one needs to be aware of the fact that each item in Denzinger's *Enchiridion Symbolorum* is culturally mediated. The third division, theological doctrines, arises from the need to have a systematic discourse about God. Lonergan states "Systematic theology sought to put order and coherence into the mass of materials assembled from scripture and tradition."[219] The fourth division concerns methodology and requires the theologian to ask "what one is doing when one is doing theology," and the answer, according to Lonergan, "must envisage not only the Christian encounter with God but also the historicity of Christian witness, the diversity of human cultures, the differentiations of human consciousness."[220] Lonergan then describes a methodological doctrine as that which focuses its reflections on theology and theologies. He notes that it is not for methodological doctrine to determine content, but it is up to the theologians to determine how to proceed.

Lonergan states that, by doctrines, he means "theological doctrines reached by the application of a method that distinguishes functional specialties and uses the functional specialty, foundations, to select doctrines from among the multiple choices presented by the functional specialty, dialectic."[221] Gregson defines doctrines as "the judgments of fact and of value which we make from the stance we have taken in Foundations."[222] Building on the new horizons established in foundations, doctrines are the affirmations made, in

---

[219] Ibid., 297.
[220] Ibid.
[221] Ibid., 298.
[222] Gregson, "Theological Method and Theological Collaboration II," 106.

authenticity, concerning truths and values, by an individual or by a group.

Doctrines help the theologian to determine where he or she stands on a particular issue, going beyond merely what one's ecclesial communion defines as a definitive doctrine. As in all the functional specialties, each builds on the other. Gregson illustrates this point by using the example of women's ordination. He writes:

> The content of a Doctrine arises from the issues one has re-flected on and evaluated in Dialectic. For instance, if the issue a theologian was considering was the contemporary issue in Roman Catholicism about the ordination of women, he or she would have posed the pertinent questions in Research, Interpretation, and History on that subject. What do we dis-cover from Scripture on this question? Is the question explic-itly addressed or even implicitly addressed? What roles have women had in the Church in the various periods of history? Has the question of ordination ever been explicitly ad-dressed? If so, how authoritative in the tradition was the an-swer? Has the growing equality of women in every aspect of society changed the context of the question or shed new light on it?[223]

Faced with this question, aware of culture and historicity, the theo-logian employs the theological specialty, dialectics, when arriving at his or her weighed evaluation. In the specialty of foundations, he or

---

[223] Ibid., 107.

she addresses any and all new horizons realized and finally, doctrines "would be the affirmations that the theologian would now make on this subject, after he or she has personally examined all of the facts and values involved."[224]

Lonergan reminds the theologian that understanding the cultural and intellectual context of a doctrine's formulation is crucial. He writes: "Doctrines that really are assimilated bear the stamp of those that assimilate them, and the absence of such an imprint would point to a merely perfunctory assimilation."[225] Marking a shift from a classicist understanding of culture to an empiricist concept, Lonergan begins to describe the stages of Western culture.[226] He is clearly against any theological apprehension of doctrine that is not both dialectic and historical. He writes: "What is opposed to the historicity of the dogmas is, not their permanence, but classicist assumptions and achievements…What ended classicist assumptions was critical history."[227]

---

[224] Ibid.

[225] Lonergan, *Method in Theology*, 300-301.

[226] Ibid., 301. He describes the classicist's view of culture as "the opposite of barbarism. It was a matter of acquiring and assimilating the tastes and skills, the ideals, virtues, and ideas, that were pressed upon one in a good home and through a curriculum in the liberal arts. It stressed not facts but values. It could not but claim to be universalist" (Ibid.).

[227] Ibid., 326. Lafontaine (54) notes that Lonergan also makes this point later in his life: "Only a theology structured by method can assimilate the somewhat recently accepted hermeneutic and historical methods and it alone has room for developing doctrines and developing theologies. The key task, then, in contemporary Catholic theology is to replace the shattered thoughtforms associated with eternal truths and logical ideals with new thoughtforms that accord with the dynamics of development and the

In describing Western Christianity, Lonergan begins to offer a series of differentiations of consciousness in the tradition. Accordingly, he lists them as "the reinterpretation of symbolic apprehension,... [the] philosophic purification of biblical anthropomorphism,... the occasional use of systematic meaning,... systematic theological doctrine,... church doctrine dependent on systematic theological doctrine, and... the complexities of contemporary development."[228]

In his analysis of Lonergan's work, Gregson details three stages of Western culture. The first he describes as a common sense stage, using symbolic and anthropomorphic language. He describes this stage as "when things are spoken of in direct relation to ourselves."[229] The second is described as a post-biblical stage, influenced by Greek cultural and thought. Gregson summarizes Lonergan's thought:

> The question with regard to the Trinity in this stage is not who are God the Father, Jesus Christ, and the Spirit as we experience them, but who are they in themselves? It is in such a world of thought that the questions and answers with regard to person and nature in the Trinity and in Christ were formulated by Church councils. These questions had not been asked in the Bible, but once the Christian Church took

---

concrete style of method" (Lonergan, "Philosophy and Theology," *A Second Collection*, eds. W. F. J. Ryan and B. J. Tyrell (Philadelphia: The Westminster Press, 1974), 202).

[228] Lonergan, *Method in Theology*, 305-306.

[229] Gregson, "Theological Method and Theological Collaboration II," 108.

root in the Hellenic world, they were inevitable questions. And if Christianity was to become integral to and grow within that culture, those questions needed to be answered.[230]

The present age, in the contemporary cultural context, is the third stage. Advancing from Greek thought, the world has realized that many things once thought certain are now only probable. Science and research have advanced and "Necessity has given way to probability and interest in method has, therefore, increased."[231] In this shift from a classicist mindset, the human being has realized the role that culture and history play in the formation of the world. This change in horizon, according to Lonergan, has "come about in the last four centuries and a half. They modify man's image of himself in his world, his science and his conception of science, his history and his conception of history, his philosophy and his conception of philosophy. They involve three basic differentiations of consciousness, and all three are quite beyond the horizon of ancient Greece and medieval Europe."[232]

All this changes the manner in which one views the development of a doctrine. Aware of the need to have moved from a classicist worldview in this examination, Lonergan writes:

---

[230] Ibid.
[231] Ibid., 109.
[232] Lonergan, *Method in Theology*, 317.

To determine the starting-point, the process, the end-result of any particular development of doctrine calls for an exact historical investigation. To determine the legitimacy of any development calls for evaluational history; one has to ask whether or not the process was under the guidance of intel-lectual, moral, and religious conversion. But the deeper issue is the more general question that asks how it is that develop-ments are possible. How is it that mortal man can develop what he would not know unless God had revealed it?[233]

Lonergan's answer involves the differentiation of consciousness of the authentic individual. Raymond Lafontaine explains: "Lonergan's argument is based on the observation that both individuals and com-munities operate within different realms of meaning; the infant's world of immediacy, the adult realm of common sense, and the more highly differentiated realms of theory, scholarship, art, interiority, and transcendence."[234] This differentiation in consciousness occurs, according to Lonergan, "…when it develops its own language, its own distinct mode of apprehension, and its own cultural, social, or professional group speaking in that fashion and apprehending in that manner."[235] Because of the differentiation of consciousness, be-cause of each human being's development being different, "legiti-mate pluralism in faith expressions, religious language, and theolog-ical systems may be attributed to the presence or absence of the other

---

[233] Ibid., 302.

[234] Lafontaine, *The Development of a Moral Doctrine*, 41.

[235] Lonergan, *Method in Theology*, 41.

five differentiations of consciousness"[236]; likewise, radical pluralism arises from "the presence or absence of intellectual, moral, or religious conversion."[237] Aware of the need for conversion in both the individual and the community, Lonergan writes: "Finally, this series contributes not a little to an understanding of the development of doctrines, for doctrines have meaning within contexts, the ongoing discovery of mind changes the contexts, and so, if the doctrines are to retain their meaning within the new contexts, they have to be recast."[238]

"A theology mediates between a cultural matrix and the significance and role of a religion in that matrix,"[239] Lonergan famously wrote. Theology, by its very nature, is contextual. Doctrine expression needs to be able to effectively communicate the truths of the faith to every age and culture, while all the while still remaining true to the content of the faith. Lonergan writes:

> ...if the Gospel is to be preached to all nations...still it is not to be preached in the same manner to all. If one is to communicate with persons of another culture, one must use the resources of their culture. To use simply the resources of one's own culture is not to communicate with the other but to remain locked up in one's own. At the same time, it is not enough simply to employ the resources of the other culture. One must do so creatively...Doctrines that really are

---

[236] Lafontaine, *The Development of a Moral Doctrine*, 41.
[237] Lonergan, *Method in Theology*, 276.
[238] Ibid., 305
[239] Ibid., xi.

assimilated bear the stamp of those that assimilate them, and the absence of such an imprint would point to a merely per-functory assimilation.[240]

Vernon Gregson notes that Lonergan wrote this chapter on doctrine for the International Theological Commission. It is important to note the warning given by Lonergan in this chapter concerning the need to understand context in doctrinal expression: "...no one should pass judgment on matters he does not understand, and no one with a less or a differently differentiated consciousness is capable of understanding accurately what is said by a person with a more fully differentiated consciousness."[241]

The Seventh Functional Specialty: Systematics

The seventh functional specialty is systematics. It is the second phase of theology and operates under the transcendental precept-"Be intelligent!" This functional specialty is concerned above all with understanding. Lonergan explains: "systematics, is concerned with promoting an understanding of the realities affirmed in the previous specialty, doctrines."[242] In many ways, this specialty is the "middle child" of this second phase theological system. It helps to articulate what was stated in the sixth functional specialty, doctrines, and

---

[240] Ibid., 300-301.
[241] Ibid., 330.
[242] Ibid., 335.

prepares one to communicate, the eighth functional specialty, to the culture and context in which the theologian finds himself or herself.

Lonergan begins his explanation of this functional specialty by describing its function. He is building on his work done in *Verbum* and *Insight* concerning the two operations of the intellect. *Insight* largely expands on Lonergan's work in *Verbum*. Lonergan does not have many novel additions to his earlier work but offers a clarification of his own thought that comes from the maturity of his research and reading. Working out of his Thomistic roots and challenged by his students' interest in contemporary philosophy, *Insight* offers Lonergan's clearest explanations of the levels of consciousness. As in all of Lonergan's thought, it is an invitation to go deeper, to not remain on the surface level, but to explore what it means to be the knower and to know how and what is knowable.

Lonergan makes this distinction between understanding and judgement and states: "…one is led to conceive understanding as the source not only of definitions but also of hypotheses, while it is by judgment that is known the existence of what has been defined, the verification of what a hypothesis proposes."[243]

Lonergan describes the danger, since medieval times, of the creation of "two theologies," a natural theology taught in the philosophy tract and "a further systematic or speculative theology concerned with an orderly presentation of the mysteries of faith."[244] "Misleading" and "weakening"[245] theology, this separation proves to Lonergan

---

[243] Ibid., 335.

[244] Ibid., 337.

[245] Ibid. He writes: "It weakened natural theology for abstruse philosophic concepts lose nothing of their validity and can gain enormously in

the necessity for methodological theology. He states: "The aim of systematics is not to increase certitude but to promote understanding."[246] The attempt in theology to have any systemic explanation leads Lonergan to declare:

> Our present concern is with doctrines and systematics. Both aim at understanding the truth, but they do so in different manners. Doctrines aims at a clear and distinct affirmation of religious realities: its principal concern is the truth of such an affirmation; its concern to understand is limited to the clarity and distinctness of its affirmation. On the other hand, systematics aims at an understanding of the religious realities affirmed by doctrines. It wants its understanding to be true, for it is not a pursuit of misunderstanding. At the same time, it is fully aware that its understanding is bound to be imperfect, merely analogous, commonly no more than probable.[247]

Gregson gives a concrete example of Lonergan's understanding of the role of systematics. He uses a Christological example from Lonergan's *De Verbo Incarnato*:

---

acceptability when they are associated with their religious equivalents. It weakened systematic theology for the separation prevents the presentation of systematics as the Christian prolongation of what man can begin to know by his native powers"(Ibid.).

[246] Ibid., 336.
[247] Ibid., 349.

That Jesus brings salvation to humankind through his death and resurrection is a basic Christian doctrine. But that teaching has given rise over the centuries to many understandings (different Systematics) about how that takes place. A number of those understandings are both fantastic and grotesque…Here we have two of God's attributes in conflict with one another.[248]

Summarizing Lonergan's approach, which Lonergan called "the law of the cross,"[249] Gregson writes:

Lonergan proposes a quite different Christian understanding of the dynamics of salvation. (1) Jesus dies because human beings reject him and his message and put him to death. This statement summarizes the facts of the biblical account. (2) Jesus by the manner of his death, his submission and his love, and by his forgiveness of his killers transforms the apparent victory of evil over good into the moral triumph of good over evil. (3) God confirms this victory of Jesus by Jesus' resurrection appearances to the apostles and disciples. (4) The

---

[248] Gregson, "Theological Method and Theological Collaboration II," 111-112.

[249] Lonergan, *De Verbo Incarnato*, 524 as quoted in Gregson, "Theological Method and Theological Collaboration II," 112. Lonergan's soteriological doctrine states: "God wisely decided and lovingly chose to take away the evils of the human race not by an act of power but by transforming those evils into a supreme good through the working of a just and mysterious law of the cross" (Ibid).

disciples and we ourselves see starkly the thrust and the ug-
liness of evil (sin) in its power to kill Jesus, God's anointed.
(5) We are moved by the power of Jesus' example and by its
confirmation by God to identify with Jesus in overcoming
evil with good in our own lives.[250]

From this soteriological/Christological example, Gregson then
articulates Lonergan's concept of systematics. In the first place, Lonergan articulates the lived experience that a Christian has in contem-
plating the cross. One is able to go beyond a theory of penal satisfaction or substitution to an understanding that "God sends his Son to
us; we take him into our hands and we see him transform our evil
into good, and, in the process, transform our understanding of our
human task and our challenge in living it."[251] Second, the mystery of
our salvation challenges the Christian with its complex "drama of
values,"[252] to make a personal response to Jesus' sacrifice and victory.
Third, Gregson notes that Lonergan's interpretation of the paschal
mystery has an openness to a "universalist interpretation," such that
it constitutes a call for all Christians to work for the transformation
of evil into good.[253] Fourth, Lonergan's soteriology challenges the
Christian to an understanding of the interiority of salvation as grace.
Gregson notes: "It is the gifted transformation of our decisional consciousness by which, in response to the loving death of Jesus, we are

---

[250] Gregson, "Theological Method and Theological Collaboration II,"
112.
[251] Ibid., 112-113.
[252] Ibid., 113.
[253] Ibid.

empowered to respond to the evil which confronts us with forgiveness and love."[254] Finally, Gregson states that Lonergan's law of the cross "shows the powerful relevance of the death of Jesus to the power of evil in the world."[255] The Christian, therefore, should realize that it is his or her role to promote progress and reverse decline.

Lonergan spends much time distinguishing between doctrine and systematics and clarifying exactly what systematic theology is. He mentions again that "Doctrines aims at a clear and distinct affirmation of religious realities: its principal concern is the truth of such an affirmation; its concern to understand is limited to the clarity and distinctness of its affirmation."[256] Systematics, as previously mentioned, is concerned with understanding.

Humorously, Lonergan describes the "accusations" against systematic theology, namely that it is "speculative, irreligious, fruitless, elitist, irrelevant."[257] To all of these pejoratives concerning systematics, Lonergan responds that each of them is true if systematic theology loses sight of its nature and its absolute need to communicate the truths of the faith within a proper cultural context.[258]

Lonergan describes both continuity and development as present in this functional specialty. A major factor also is revision because of the very contextual nature of theology. He writes: "...because a theology is the product not simply of a religion but of a religion within

---

[254] Ibid.

[255] Ibid.

[256] Lonergan, *Method in Theology*, 349.

[257] Ibid., 350.

[258] Ibid., 351.

a given cultural context, theological revisions may have their origin, not primarily in theological, but rather in cultural developments."[259]

Above all else, Lonergan emphasizes the important pastoral nature of systematics. A major aspect of fundamental theology is making revelation credible. This is the functional specialty that addresses the concerns of those who struggle to make their faith credible and relevant in the contemporary world. Lonergan writes:

> The ongoing contexts within which mystery is adored and adoration is explained are anything but free from problems...now problems are so numerous that many do not know what to believe. They are not unwilling to believe. They know what church doctrines are. But they want to know what church doctrines could possibly mean. Their question is the question to be met by systematic theology.[260]

The Eighth Functional Specialty: Communications

The eighth and final of the functional specialties, communications, corresponds to the transcendental precept "Be attentive!" As with all the functional specialties, it builds on all of its immediate predecessors. Lonergan succinctly phrases this:

> After *research*, which assembles the data thought relevant, and *interpretation*, which ascertains their meaning, and

---

[259] Ibid., 353.
[260] Ibid., 345.

history, which finds meanings incarnate in deeds and movements, and *dialectic*, which investigates the conflicting con-
clusions of historians, interpreters, researchers, and *foundations*, which objectifies the horizon effected by intellectual,
moral, and religious conversion, and *doctrines*, which uses
foundations as a guide in selecting from the alternatives presented by dialectic, and *systematics*, which seeks an ultimate
clarification of the meaning of doctrine, there finally comes
our present concern with the eighth functional specialty,
communications.[261]

Lonergan believes that, in communications, "theological reflection
bears fruit."[262] The theologian has the obligation to engage in communication. It is in this functional specialty that the theoretical and
practical insights gained from all the functional specialties are exhibited. To explain communications, Lonergan builds on some of his
thoughts from *Insight*. He writes:

> …[Communication is] a work of art; and it has at its disposal
> not merely all the resources of language but also the support
> of modulated tone and changing volume, the eloquence of
> facial expression, the emphasis of gestures, the effectiveness
> of pauses, the suggestiveness of questions, the significance of
> omissions…[I]t can also take on all the delicacy and subtlety,
> all the rapidity and effectiveness, with which one incarnate

---

[261] Ibid., 355.
[262] Ibid.

intelligence can communicate its grasp to another by grasp-
ing what the other has yet to grasp and what act or sound or
sign would make him grasp it…[263]

It is in communications that the theologian uses his mandate to
teach.[264] It is in teaching, in this communication of insight, that
"…the discoveries and inventions of individuals pass into the possession of many, to be checked against their experience, to undergo the
scrutiny of their further questions, to be modified by their improve-
ments."[265] With this thought, Lonergan is aware of the recurrent process of method in theology and knows, "What is Communications
for the present generation, however, becomes the data for Research
for the next generation."[266]

Communications transmits meaning and is constitutive of culture. Religion becomes theology when mediated through a cultural
matrix. Communicated meaning and values constitute community:

---

[263] Lonergan, *Insight*, 200-201.

[264] Ibid., 197. Commenting on teaching, Lonergan writes: "(T)eaching
is the communication of insight. It throws out the clues, the pointed hints,
that lead to insight. It cajoles attention to drive away the distracting images
that stand in insight's way. It puts the further questions that reveal the need
of further insights to modify and complement the acquired store. It has
grasped the strategy of developing intelligence, and so begins from the simple to advance to the more complex. Deliberately and explicitly, all this is
done by professional teachers that know their job" (Ibid., 197-198).

[265] Ibid., 198.

[266] Gregson, "Theological Method and Collaboration: II," 115.

The message announces what Christians are to believe, what they are to become, what they are to do. Its meaning, then, is at once cognitive, constitutive, effective. It is cognitive inasmuch as the message tells what is to be believed. It is constitutive inasmuch as it crystallizes the hidden inner gift of love into overt Christian fellowship. It is effective inasmuch as it directs Christian service to human society to bring about the kingdom of God.[267]

Lonergan explains, "Community is not just an aggregate of individuals within a frontier"[268] but derives its nature from common meaning. Common meaning, in turn, comes from "a common field of experience."[269] Without common meaning, without shared goals, values, and policies, progress easily regresses into decline.

In common meaning, people share the "same cognitive, constitutive, and effective meanings."[270] However, over time meanings can develop, and this shift in meaning has an effect on the nature of community. Lonergan writes:

As common meaning constitutes community, so divergent meaning divides it. Such division may amount to no more

---

[267] Lonergan, *Method in Theology*, 362.

[268] Ibid., 356.

[269] Ibid. Lonergan explains "Such common meaning is doubly constitutive. In each individual it is constitutive of the individual as a member of the community. In the group of individuals it is constitutive of the community" (Ibid., 357).

[270] Ibid., 357.

than a diversity of culture and the stratification of individuals into classes of higher and lower competence. The serious division is the one that arises from the presence and absence of intellectual, moral, or religious conversion. For a man is his true self inasmuch as he is self-transcending. Conversion is the way to self-transcendence. Inversely, man is alienated from his true self inasmuch as he refuses self-transcendence, and the basic form of ideology is the self-justification of alienated man.[271]

"(T)he divided community, their conflicting actions, and the messy situation are headed for disaster."[272] Communications, the basis of community and society, seeks to avoid the "disaster" that is decline. In the creation of states and societies, communications must be clearly articulated. This necessitates the need for "procedures" and "agencies," which are available to "train personnel, offer roles and set tasks within already understood and accepted styles and modes of cooperation."[273] Lonergan writes:

…the ideal basis of society is community. Without a large measure of community, human society and sovereign states cannot function. Without a constant renewal of community, the measure of community already enjoyed easily is squandered. There are needed, then, individuals and groups and,

---

[271] Ibid.
[272] Ibid., 358.
[273] Ibid., 361.

in the modern world, organizations that labor to persuade people to intellectual, moral, and religious conversion and that work systematically to undo the mischief brought about by alienation and ideology. Among such bodies should be the Christian church…[274]

Lonergan's attention then turns to the Church and what constitutes the Church's role within society. As always, he begins by distinguishing what the Church is: "The Christian church is the community that results from the outer communication of Christ's message and from the inner gift of God's love."[275] Practical theology, therefore, above all else, involves the communication of the Love that is God in Christ to the world. Lonergan states the message that is Christ's "announces what Christians are to believe, what they are to become, what they are to do."[276] The meaning of the message, like all meanings, is cognitive, constitutive, and effective.[277]

In communicating the Christian message, those entrusted with this task must know it and live it. The horizon of all those who minister in the Catholic Church must know the culture and the context of all those to whom they minister. Lonergan states: "They must

---

[274] Ibid.

[275] Ibid., 361.

[276] Ibid., 362.

[277] Ibid. Lonergan writes: "It is cognitive inasmuch as the message tells what is to be believed. It is constitutive inasmuch as it crystallizes the hidden inner gift of love into overt Christian fellowship. It is effective inasmuch as it directs Christian service to human society to bring about the kingdom of God" (Ibid.).

grasp the virtual resources of that culture and that language, and they must use those virtual resources creatively so that the Christian message becomes, not disruptive of the culture, not an alien patch superimposed upon it, but a line of development within the culture."[278] Moving from a classicist mindset, he or she who teaches and preaches the Christian message, aware of the differentiations of consciousness, realizes that he or she is communicating not only faith but also culture.

Lonergan believes that it is communications that constitute community and "conversely, community constitutes and perfects itself through communication."[279] The Church, therefore, needs to recognize its two-fold nature: as a "structured process," training personnel, assigning roles, etc., while at the same time, it is an "out-going process," and "It exists not just for itself but for mankind. Its aim is the realization of the kingdom of God not only within its own organization but in the whole of human society and not only in the after life but also in this life."[280]

The Church also is a redemptive process, aware of the sins of its members and the sins of the world. Lonergan states:

Sin is alienation from man's authentic being, which is self-transcendence, and sin justifies itself by ideology. As alienation and ideology are destructive of community, so the self-sacrificing love that is Christian charity reconciles alienated

---

[278] Ibid.

[279] Ibid., 363.

[280] Ibid., 363-364.

man to his true being, and undoes the mischief initiated by alienation and consolidated by ideology.[281]
In order to accomplish its task of promoting progress and reversing decline, the functional specialty of communications also involves the dialogue with men and women of other ecclesial communities and with other branches of learning. [282] Going beyond a mere condemnation of decline, the Church, in dialogue with the secular sciences, can promote progress for all humankind.[283]

An Underdeveloped Second Phase - A Need for Completion

Most scholars of Lonergan's life and work believe that *Method in Theology*, although a theological breakthrough, especially in the creation of the functional specialties, is a text that is largely incomplete and underbalanced. There are two reasons generally given as to why this is the case. The first is Lonergan's own interests in the first phase of theology more so than the second phase. Michael Shute comments:

---

[281] Ibid., 364.
[282] Ibid., 367-368. He notes, "… division resides mainly in the cognitive meaning of the Christian message. The constitutive meaning and the effective meaning are matters on which most Christians very largely agree. Such agreement, however, needs expression and, while we await common cognitive agreement, the possible expression is collaboration in fulfilling the redemptive and constructive roles of the Christian church in human society" (Ibid., 368).
[283] Ibid., 366-367.

Lonergan was an outstanding dialectical thinker...Beyond this, he recognized the profoundly personal element in dialectic which challenges one's own corrupted thinking...The later chapters of *Method in Theology*, however, reveal a weakness with respect to his thinking forward in concrete fantasy towards a future reality...He understood that the withdrawal from practicality was for the sake of a return. He left a sketch of the way back, but overall he left to others the task of working out a strategy of return.[284]

The other school of thought notes that Lonergan was quite ill when he was writing *Method in Theology*. Frederick Crowe notes: "*Method* does suffer in comparison with *Insight*. It is schematic in style almost to the point of being laconic, and the content lacks the leisurely sweep of its great predecessor...one feels that the Lonergan of presurgery times would have greatly expanded them."[285]

There is no one who has taken the work begun by Lonergan in *Insight* and *Method in Theology* forward more than Robert Doran. In chapter four, Doran's achievements, all of which have their roots in Lonergan's thought, will be detailed and explored, especially Doran's addition of the psychic conversion.

---

[284] Michael Shute, *Lonergan's Discovery of the Science of Economics* (Toronto: University of Toronto Press, 2010), 238. Particularly underdeveloped is the eighth functional specialty, communications, which is given only fourteen pages by Lonergan.

[285] Crowe, *Lonergan*, 107.

Chapter Four

The Completion of Lonergan's Work through Robert Doran

In the construction of one's own theology, theologians cannot help but build, not only on the fonts of revelation, namely, Sacred Scripture and Sacred Tradition, but also on the formulations of theologians who have preceded them. From Augustine to Bonaventure to Aquinas onward, the genealogy of a theologian is an important hermeneutical key to understanding a particular theologian's life works.

John M. Dadosky summarizes the task and method of Robert M. Doran's theology succinctly:

> Bernard Lonergan states in the Epilogue of *Insight* that he spent years reaching up to the mind of Aquinas and it was the *reaching* that changed him profoundly. Robert M. Doran, SJ spent over the last 40 years of his life reaching up to the mind of Lonergan. To say that the reaching has changed him may not adequately capture the influence that Lonergan has had, not only on Doran's own life, but on the colleagues who have benefitted from the bounty of Doran's labors.[1]

---

[1] John D. Dadosky, "Introduction," in *Meaning and History in Systematic Theology: Essays in Honor of Robert M. Doran, SJ*, ed. John D. Dadosky (Milwaukee: Marquette University Press, 2009), 9.

Robert Doran, as a theologian, has expanded on Bernard Lonergan's foundations and, in doing so, has created his own unique systematic theology that not only fulfills the need for a practical, pastoral implementation of Lonergan's theology but also offers an interdisciplinary approach that weds depth psychology and history to systematic theology.

Psychic Conversion: Doran's Context for the Psychic Conversion

Doran has applied Lonergan's methodology to Jung's depth psychology, beginning with his doctoral thesis, *Subject and Psyche* (1975), and continuing with his publication of his work, *Psychic Conversion and Theological Foundations*, in 1981.[2] This application of Lonergan and the articulation of a fourth conversion, the psychic, will be studied in greater detail in this chapter.

Doran's work in *Subject and Psyche* attempts to demonstrate Lonergan's shift from primary cognitional analysis to that of intentionality analysis and then applies it to the area of depth psychology and the human psyche. Doran then attempts to identify the level of human consciousness that concerns itself with the issue of value, the *notio valoris* (the human good).[3] Noting that "Values are primordially apprehended in feelings, and feelings are ascertainable, identifiable, through symbols,"[4] Doran uses both

---

[2] See Robert M. Doran, *Psychic Conversion and Theological Foundations*, Second Edition (Milwaukee: Marquette University Press, 2006).

[3] Robert M. Doran, *Subject and Psyche: Ricoeur, Jung, and the Search for Foundations* (Lanham, MD: University of America Press, 1980), iii.

[4] Ibid.

Lonergan's intentionality analysis and Ricoeur's symbolic philosophy to transcend Jungian analytical psychology and to offer a
greater understanding of the individual's symbolic interiority.

Doran's Concept of the Psychic Conversion

At the beginning of his work, *Psychic Conversion and Theological
Foundations*, Doran establishes his groundwork for the creation of
his "methodical Christian theology:"[5]

In brief, a theology will be methodical to the extent that its
practitioners submit their cognitive, affective, moral, religious, and Christian consciousness to explanatory differentiation in the mode of interiority, thereby recovering with
structural precision the path and the immanent intelligibility
of their own search for direction in the movement of life, and
that they ground their theology in the discoveries they have
made and verified along that path.[6]

Doran acknowledges that he is building on a framework provided
by Lonergan. He writes in *Theology and the Dialectics of History*:
"(T)he present book, while not out of harmony with Lonergan's
thought, reflects certain emphases and even clarifications that either add to what he has said or draw out implications of his work

---

[5] Doran, *Psychic Conversion and Theological Foundations*, 19.
[6] Ibid.

in ways that he did not stress."[7] Like his mentor, Bernard Lonergan, Doran believes that the theologian, in order to truly accomplish his task of being the one who helps "mediate between religion and the role of religion in that cultural matrix,"[8] must be self-authentic. Before an understanding of psychic conversion can be successful, Doran first begins to explain, in a "disengaged manner," what the foundational reality is in what conversion is seeking to objectify. Elizabeth Murray understands Doran's work in his concept of psychic conversion as a "masterful study of the problem of sustained development."[9] Describing Doran's work in this field, she writes:

> He writes of the 'movement of life,' the natural internal dynamism that would move us to further development and creativity, and the various obstacles to this dynamism. The dialectical obstacles to growth are both socio-historical and psychological. The subject develops in an inherited, socio-historical context already riddled with the effects of bias and the surd of sin. Insofar as one inadvertently adopts the inauthenticity of one's world, one's psychological development may be similarly distorted. The psychological

---

[7] Robert M. Doran, *Theology and the Dialectics of History* (Toronto: University of Toronto Press, 1990), 8.

[8] Lonergan, *Method in Theology*, 9.

[9] Elizabeth A. Murray, "Unmasking the Censor," in *Meaning and History in Systematic Theology: Essays in Honor of Robert M. Doran, SJ*, ed. John D. Dadosky (Milwaukee, Wisconsin: Marquette University Press, 2009), 423.

aberration of dramatic bias disorients and stultifies the movement of life. It is within the complex framework of these dialectical obstacles that Doran introduces the concept of *psychic conversion*. He focuses on the role that psychic conversion has in conjunction with the 'healing vector' of God's love in liberating the immanent 'creative vector.'[10]

Doran states, "the notion of psychic conversion will enable us to make use of the resources of depth psychology as aids toward the emergence and clarification of the subject in Christ Jesus, that subject who, as theologian, is also the radical foundational reality in theology."[11] Doran, in his interdisciplinary nature, describes how the knowledge and use of depth psychology are essential to the discernment of spirits and the growth of human self-authenticity. He writes:

Depth psychology would illuminate dimensions of consciousness in which there is experienced the very movement of life, the passionateness of being, in which it is our task to find direction. What the Christian tradition has called discernment is the search for direction in the movement of life. The experience of the movement provides data that, if we know how to interpret them, are indications as to whether or not we are finding or missing the direction. The ability to

---

[10] Ibid.

[11] Doran, *Theology and the Dialectics of History*, 42.

read those indications is obviously, then, a great help to discernment, and the science of depth psychology can be of great importance in helping us gain that ability.[12]

Doran acknowledges the impact of the "great architects"[13] of depth psychology, namely, Freud and Jung. He states that his criticisms of these two psychologists lie primarily in their understanding that our acts of meaning and objectives are "radical ciphers for discovering what we are."[14] Doran recognizes that Freud and Jung did not have a completely proper understanding of human thinking and deciding and, more importantly, did not grasp "the movements of breakthrough and grace that effect our entrance into a state of being in love and that maintain us in a relative fidelity to self-transcendence as a way of life."[15] Lonergan's concept of operations (inquiry, insight, conceptualization, formulation, reflective understanding, judgment of fact, deliberation, judgment of value, decision, and acts of love) fulfills the framework given by the depth psychologists.

The topics of bias, psychic conversion, and the dialectics of

<hr>

[12] Ibid., 42-43. Doran will use his connection between Lonergan's theology and depth psychology and apply it to the Spiritual Exercises of St. Ignatius of Loyola in several articles, especially "Ignatian Themes in the Thought of Bernard Lonergan: Revisiting a Topic that Deserves Further Reflection," in *Lonergan Workshop 19*, ed. Fred Lawrence (Boston College, 2006), 83-106, and "Ignatian Themes in the Thought of Bernard Lonergan," *Toronto Journal of Theology* 22, no. 1 (2006): 39-54.

[13] Doran, *Theology and the Dialectics of History*, 45.

[14] Ibid.

[15] Ibid.

growth in history will each be discussed in the context of Doran's work.

Bias

In order to understand exactly what Doran means by psychic conversion, one needs to return to Doran's roots in Lonergan, both in *Insight* and in *Method in Theology*. The concept of bias, according to Lonergan, needs to be primary in our minds. In *Insight*, we recall that Lonergan declares:

Just as insight can be desired, so too it can be unwanted. Besides the love of light, there can be a love of darkness. If prepossessions and prejudices notoriously vitiate theoretical investigations, much more easily can elementary passions bias understanding in practical and personal matters.[16]

As such, there are different types and levels of bias. On the level of the individual subject, one can suffer from dramatic bias. Lonergan states that the human psyche has a two-fold responsibility: first, it registers the sensations upon which the spirit reflects, and second, it forms images in the mind into which the spirit spurs acts of insight. Dramatic bias causes the subject not to be able to properly process the formation of images in the psyche and thus not be able to understand the situation properly. This cognitive distortion primarily occurs on the level of the unconscious.

---

[16] Lonergan, *Insight*, 214.

The next level of bias is that of individual bias. This is when a subject makes a clear and intentional decision to surrender to the ego and to reject conscience. Lonergan, in describing the ego, states, "Egoism is neither mere spontaneity nor pure intelligence but an interference of spontaneity with the development of intelligence. With remarkable acumen one solves one's own problems. With startling modesty one does not venture to raise the relevant further questions."[17] In many ways, this egoism is an act of selfishness and a lack of true maturity. This failure in self-authenticity affects not only the individual but also the group. Lonergan describes this societal bias: "We reinforce our love of truth with a practicality that is equivalent to an obscurantism. We correct old evils with a passion that mars the new good."[18] Lonergan breaks this societal bias down into two types: a group bias and a general bias. The group bias is a gathering of likeminded individuals, bound together as "functional groups," linked by "imagination and emotion, sentiment and confidence, familiarity and loyalty," all to the neglect of the common good.[19] This group bias is a "social surd,"[20] according to Lonergan and aids in the creation of a "shorter cycle [of decline]."[21]

General bias, according to Lonergan, is much more dangerous

---

[17] Ibid., 245.

[18] Ibid., 91.

[19] Ibid., 248.

[20] Ibid., 255. The term "surd" is appropriated by Lonergan from the field of mathematics, where it is used to describe irrational numbers.

[21] Lonergan, *Insight*, 252.

and can lead to a "longer cycle of decline."[22] He writes:

> For the flight from understanding blocks the insights that concrete situations demand. There follow unintelligent policies and inept courses of action. The situation deteriorates to demand still further insights, and as they are blocked, policies become more unintelligent and action more inept. What is worse, the deteriorating situation seems to provide the uncritical, biased mind with factual evidence in which the bias is claimed to be verified. So in ever increasing measure intelligence comes to be regarded as irrelevant to practical living.[23]

General bias is both individual and collective and is the "stubborn refusal of people of common sense to admit the validity of any other realm of knowledge other than their own."[24] This common-sense bias desires to "rationalize its limitations by engendering a conviction that other forms of human knowledge are useless or doubtfully valid."[25] General bias acts against the individual's innate pure desire to know.

The Psychic Level

Murray describes the psychic level as that which "underlies the

---

[22] Ibid., 264.
[23] Ibid., 8.
[24] Whelan, *Redeeming History*, 92.
[25] Lonergan, *Insight*, 251.

spiritual levels of conscious intentionality, the level of intelligent consciousness, rational consciousness, and rational self-consciousness or moral consciousness."[26] This psychic level, "the level of sense, perception, imagination, memory, desires, and feelings,"[27] operates on the conscious and unconscious level and helps to organize the unconscious neurological level. Operating not necessarily on the level of conscious intentionality, as do intellectual, moral, and spiritual conversions, this psychic conversion is not a decision and thus does not operate on the fourth level of consciousness but on the first. Doran states, "Psychic conversion is a transformation of the psychic component of what Freud calls 'the censor' from a repressive to a constructive agency in a person's development."[28] Doran holds that the psychic censor operates on the unconscious neural level and operates spontaneously; thus, psychic appropriation is determined.[29] In order to understand what Doran means by the censor, Freud's concept of the censor and Lonergan's concept of the censor will be examined prior to that of Doran's, as both Freud and Lonergan have a great impact on the development of Doran's thought.

The Psychic Censor According to Freud

The psychologist Sigmund Freud holds that a censor exists between the conscious and the unconscious mind. He develops this

---

[26] Murray, "Unmasking the Censor," 424.

[27] Ibid.

[28] Doran, *Theology and the Dialectics of History*, 59.

[29] Ibid.,142. See Murray, 424.

idea in his 1899 text, *The Interpretation of Dreams*.[30] Freud states that "*a dream is the fulfillment of a wish*,"[31] and it is the role of psychologist to interpret that dream for his client so that he or she can come to a greater self-awareness. He holds that there are two "thought-constructing agencies," conscious and unconscious, and that the censor exists on the border of the conscious and the unconscious.[32] The censor functions to "only allows what is agreeable to it to pass through and holds back everything else…what is rejected by the censorship is in a state of repression."[33] The dreaming state permits thoughts, feelings, wishes, and desires that would be suppressed in the conscious state to flow more freely in this unconscious state; however, there is still "a systematic process of distortion and disguise which renders the content of a dream obscure."[34] Between the repression present in the conscious mind and the relaxation of censorship in the unconscious mind, a compromise develop that makes the contents of dreams distorted, disguised, and obscure. The conscious mind does not generally remember the content of dreams so that it does not have to deal with the vital function of the unconscious mind in the waking state.

The unconscious mind has total access to the conscious mind. The censor, for Freud, is thus a function of consciousness. In

---

[30] Sigmund Freud, *The Interpretation of Dreams*, in *The Freud Reader*, ed. Peter Gay (New York: W.W. Norton Company, 1989).

[31] Ibid., 142.

[32] Sigmund Freud, "On Dreams," in *The Freud Reader*, ed. Peter Gay (New York: W.W. Norton Company, 1989), 165-166.

[33] Ibid., 166.

[34] Murray, "Unmasking the Censor," 427.

relating the censor to the unconscious mind, Freud notes the conscious mind has two senses: a descriptive sense, dealing with general human self-awareness, and a systematic sense, which is the area in which psychoanalysis functions.[35] As his thought progresses on the matter, Freud leaves behind the idea of the censor as a "border," a fixed location, and begins to describe psychic forces as dynamic. Moving from simply delineating conscious and unconscious, Freud adds the level of the preconscious. The preconscious may be described as "that which has been repressed, which we are not presently aware of, but yet still may become conscious if not again repressed."[36]

The censor in Freud's new development acts as the agent of differentiation between the three levels of consciousness.[37] As Freud's thought further progressed, he moved from the description of unconscious, preconscious, and conscious to that of Ego, Id, and Superego.[38] While not a complete transposition between the two different typologies,[39] it is important to note that, for Freud, the Ego, more or less, functions in the same capacity as the censor in Freud's

---

[35] Ibid., 428. In describing Freud's systematic sense, Murray writes: "The latter [(systematic sense)] is the unconscious as uncovered through the clinical phenomena of resistance and transference, and as manifested in dreams and in certain waking parapraxes, such as slips of the tongue, misreadings, slips of the pen (typos), bungled actions, etc." (Ibid.).

[36] Ibid., 429.

[37] Ibid. See Sigmund Freud, "The Unconscious," in *The Freud Reader*, ed. Peter Gay (New York: W.W. Norton Company, 1989), 578.

[38] See Sigmund Freud, "The Ego and the Id," in *The Freud Reader*, ed. Peter Gay (New York: W.W. Norton Company, 1989), 631-635.

[39] Murray, "Unmasking the Censor," 429-431.

earlier formulation. Freud states, "it exercises the censorship on dreams."[40]

Summarizing Freud's thoughts on the censor, Murray writes:

In the first typology, the censor stands as the guard or tester on the border between the Unconscious and the Conscious, and also on the border between the Preconscious and the Conscious. He describes the censor as a function of the second thought-constructing agency, that which has access to consciousness. In the second typology, the role of the censor is attributed to the Ego, to which consciousness is primarily attached but which at its outer edges is also unconscious. The function of the censor, then, is closely associated with consciousness in both typologies, that is, throughout the development of Freud's metapsychology. Yet whether the process of censorship is consciously controlled by the self-conscious ego remains unresolved. While guarding and protecting consciousness and functioning as an agent of consciousness in that sense, it nevertheless seems that censorship itself takes place behind the back of the conscious ego.[41]

Well aware of the serious critiques given to Freud's concept of censor, it nonetheless plays an important factor in the development of this concept in the thought of both Lonergan and Doran.

---

[40] Freud, "The Ego and the Id," 630.
[41] Murray, "Unmasking the Censor," 431-431.

The Psychic Censor According to Lonergan

Lonergan, in his studies of contemporary philosophy and culture, would no doubt have been aware of both Freud's concept of
the censor as well as the substantial criticism given to Freud's concept. Lonergan's understanding of the censor is "an explanatory
conjugate of the psychic level of consciousness. It functions in cor-
relation to the neural demands of the underlying unconscious level
and to the intelligent and rational (or obfuscating and biased) intentionality of the higher levels of intelligent and rational consciousness."[42] Lonergan accepts the unconscious level, but indicates that he does not intend this "unconscious" to be a region of
the psyche, but "the underlying neural level."[43] Later on in his writings, he would define the unconscious as "This twilight of what is
conscious but not objectified seems to be the meaning of what some
psychiatrists call the unconscious."[44] Lonergan applies the censor
to the tension in interaction with the conscious and unconscious
mind. Biologically, he explains, the human mind and the human
body are linked by stimuli and are connected by a "neural manifold." Lonergan writes:

In man, there is intellectual development supervening upon
psychic and psychic supervening upon organic....In the organism both the underlying manifold and the higher system

---

[42] Ibid., 438.

[43] Ibid., 433.

[44] Lonergan, *Method in Theology*, 34 no. 5.

are unconscious. In intellectual development both the under-lying manifold of sensible presentations and the higher system of insights and formulations are conscious. In psychic development the underlying neural manifold is unconscious and the supervening higher system is conscious.[45]

On each level of integration, there are "conjugates" or explanatory terms that are defined by the particular level.[46] The censor functions as an "explanatory conjugate of the psychic level on a par with impulses, affects, images, behaviors, dreams, and the processes of repression and inhibition."[47] Lonergan holds that the stimuli in the neural manifold need expression in the conscious, and images are produced as the means of expression. So that human intelligence does not become overwhelmed by all the images produced, it places a censor over exactly what stimuli can be accepted into consciousness. Lonergan exhibits his awareness of Freud's thoughts by stating: "(T)he function that excludes elements from emerging in consciousness is now familiar as Freud's censor."[48] This censor, according to Lonergan, is relaxed in sleep but repressive in the waking state.[49] The psychic censor anticipates the meaning and significance of stimuli for acts of insight without the foreknowledge of exactly what insights will arise. The censor "penetrates below the

---

[45] Lonergan, *Insight*, 492.

[46] Ibid., 102-105. See Murray, "Unmasking the Censor," 434-435, as well for a concise summary of Lonergan's thought.

[47] Murray, "Unmasking the Censor," 434.

[48] Lonergan, *Insight*, 214.

[49] Ibid., 218.

surface of consciousness to exercise its own domination and control, and to effect, prior to conscious discrimination, its own selections and arrangements."[50]

Lonergan states that the censor functions in different manners according to the different "patterns of experience" in which the human mind functions. He describes this as follows: "Besides the demands of neural processes, there also is the pattern of experience in which their demands are met; and as the elements that enter consciousness are already within a pattern, there must be exercised some preconscious selection and arrangement."[51] Lonergan describes this "pattern of experience" as "dramatic" because it is in a personal context, and the subject experiences his or her own life as a "creative work of art."[52]

Lonergan holds that the censor plays not only a role that is repressive, but is primarily also a constructive element of the human psyche.[53] What the censor permits into the consciousness is different by different individuals. How the psychic censor is able to adapt in each person indicates the prime difference between the human being and animals, which remain only on a "biological pattern of

---

[50] Ibid., 213-214.

[51] Ibid., 213.

[52] Murray, "Unmasking the Censor," 435. Lonergan writes: "Such artistry is dramatic. It is in the presence of others, and the others too are also actors in the primordial drama that the theatre only imitates" (Lonergan, *Insight*, 211).

[53] Doran would later agree with Lonergan's statement: "Primarily the censorship is constructive; it selects and arranges materials that emerge in consciousness in a perspective that gives rise to an insight" (Doran, *Theology and the Dialectics of History*, 60)

experience."[54]

Three interrelated operations are present in the dramatic pattern of experience. Present first is the stimuli that require some representation and integration in the supervening level of psychic consciousness. This desire for conscious expression is termed by Lonergan as "neural demand functions" and can be expressed in any number of ways. However, the subject needs to express at least some of them in order to not grow abnormally. Lonergan writes: "The demand functions of neural patterns and processes constitute the exigence of the organism for its conscious complement; and to violate that exigence is to invite the anguish of abnormality."[55]

The next level, that of understanding, tries to process the psychic material that has made it into the consciousness. Murray comments, "The unfettered desire to know will penetrate the underlying psychic level and even the neural level positively to seek out the patterns and images required for insight."[56] However, bias can enter into this level, and fear can block images that could be used to come to positive, creative insights.

Bias, which, at its essence, is a "refusal to understand,"[57] and can be conquered by understanding. Murray summarizes well the role of the censor in Lonergan's thought:

---

[54] Lonergan, *Insight*, 214.

[55] Ibid.

[56] Murray, "Unmasking the Censor," 436.

[57] Ibid., 437. See the work of depth psychology William Stekel in his *Technique of Analytical Psychotherapy*, trans. Eden and Cedar Paul (New York: Liveright, 1950). Lonergan was familiar with Stekel's work and mentions it in *Insight*, 224.

In both its positive and its negative functions, the censor for Lonergan is correlated to the level of intelligence. The censor prepares the psychic materials into which we have insights, and its selection is influenced by the desire to understand or by the dread of understanding, which penetrates to the underlying psychic and neural levels.[58]

It is upon this framework provided by Lonergan that Doran builds his notion of subject and psyche.

Subject and Psyche according to Doran

In "Report in a Work in Progress" (1984), Robert Doran describes the origins of his idea of psychic conversion. He writes:

> After nearly a year of wrestling with the question of how to integrate a process of psychic self-appropriation, involving a good deal of dream analysis, with the dimensions of interiorly differentiated consciousness promoted by the work of Bernard Lonergan, in February of 1973 a basic insight occurred to me that I have been laboring to articulate, develop, test, and amplify ever since. The insight was to the effect that there is a fourth aspect of foundational subjectivity, and so of conversion, beyond the three instances–intellectual, moral, and religious–whose objectification constitutes in Lonergan's work the theological functional specialty

---

[58] Murray, "Unmasking the Censor," 437.

'foundations.' I have called this fourth aspect of conversion 'psychic conversion.'[59]

Doran divides his work prior to this point into method and psychology and indicates that this is the true beginning of his work in systematic theology. Truly a disciple of Lonergan, he indicates that the first volume of his book will consider two themes: "the cultural matrix of a contemporary systematics and the meaning of integrity or authenticity within that matrix."[60] Aware that the cultural matrix in which systematic theology must deal is global, he determines that the "global cultural matrix of our age"[61] is made of "several competing and escalating sets of totalitarian ambitions":[62] first, a "progressionist myth of automatic expansion, unlimited progress, and exponential growth," exhibited more clearly in "transnational corporational capitalism,"[63] and second, "the myth of class conflict as the indispensable and infallible means to social harmony,"[64] most clearly exhibited in Marxist states. Torn between capitalism run amuck and communism gone astray, Christianity then, for Doran,

---

[59] Robert Doran, "Report on a Work in Progress," in *Theological Foundations, Volume Two: Theology and Culture*, Marquette Studies in Theology no. 9 (Milwaukee: Marquette University, 1995), 3. This essay was originally published in *Searching for Cultural Foundations*, ed. Philip McShane (Lanham, MD: University Press of America, 1984), 44-64. The years to which Doran refers are 1973-1982.

[60] Ibid., 4.

[61] Ibid.

[62] Ibid.

[63] Ibid.

[64] Ibid.

has a clear role in this new cultural matrix: to promote a "mentality that would become incarnate in alternative communities."[65] These communities, in praxis, would operate on the order of values, according to Lonergan's system, which Doran, using Lewis Mumford's term, names "world-cultural humanity."[66]

> In such a conception religious values condition the possibility of personal integrity, personal integrity conditions the possibility of genuine cultural values, such cultural values condition the possibility of a just social order, and a just social order conditions the possibility of an equitable distribution of particular goods.[67]

Doran states that the conversions, when objectified, constitute theological foundations, and this serves as the grounding of praxis in world-cultural humanity.[68] Doran believes that all his work to this

---

[65] Ibid.

[66] Ibid., 5.

[67] Ibid.

[68] Ibid., 5. In a footnote added in 1993, Doran comments that he would add "a social dimension to conversion, based on the relations among the levels of value." See footnote 7, page 28. Doran mentions that the superstructural praxis consists of an academic collaboration that is interdisciplinary and an infrastructural praxis that involves "the transformation of the myriad varieties of common sense…integrating the cosmological, anthropological, and soteriological modes of spontaneous self-understanding that constitute the authentic heritage of the various cultural traditions, and by reversing the mechanomorphic self-understanding that informs the common sense of totalitarian societies" (Ibid., 5).

point was primarily methodological and, as such, psychological, a "preface to a theology for a world-cultural humanity."[69] It is the search for authenticity in the human subject, with methodology provided by Lonergan, which gives praxis a firm hold in Doran. He backs up this methodology with "a dialectical confrontation with Jungian depth psychology."[70] The methodological aspect must precede the psychological and the psychological is, in turn, firmly rooted in a generalized empirical method provided by Lonergan. Doran states: "both of the aspects or phases of my work are a fitting preparation for my present concerns: the methodological aspect because of the transcultural structure of consciousness disengaged in Lonergan's writings, and the psychological because of the potential of Jung's insights for promoting crosscultural understanding".[71]

Psychic Self-Appropriation

Doran describes the notion of "psychic self-appropriation," a process of dream analysis that led to his understanding delineated in *Subject and Psyche*.[72] He believes that the categories created through

---

[69] Ibid., 6.

[70] Ibid.

[71] Ibid.

[72] Ibid., 7. Doran mentions that his process of dream analysis occurred with the assistance of Dr. Charles Goldsmith. In addition to *Subject and Psyche: Ricoeur, Jung, and the Search for Foundations*, please see Robert Doran, "Psychic Conversion," *The Thomist* (1977): 200-236 and "Subject, Psyche, and Theology's Foundations," *Journal of Religion* (1977): 267-287. These two articles are printed as chapters two and three, respectively,

psychic self-appropriation are foundational and are necessary in order that Lonergan's categories may truly be fulfilled. He writes, "my conviction is that the self-knowledge that is gained through psychic analysis is just as transformative as is that acquired through intentionality analysis, and that *the latter can neither supply nor substitute for the former.*"[73] Doran indicates that four new categories, essential for foundations, were discovered in his work: "second immediacy, the imaginal, psychic conversion, and the anagogic."[74]

Doran posits that, in order to give a fuller impression of the converted subject in Lonergan, it is necessary to offer psychic analysis to Lonergan's intentionality analysis. In the same manner, then, it is also necessary to form psychic analysis in Lonergan's intentionality analysis. These two forms of analysis must be seen in dialectic with each other. Jungian psychology does not sufficiently account for the foundational reality of knowledge, morality, and religion. Lonergan's categories can supply this firm foundation.

Phase One: Methodology

Doran admits that, in many ways, his work in *Subject and Psyche* was naïve. He states that he believed Jungian psychology could be integrated with Lonergan's method with "little more than a purging from Jungian thought of its at least implicit Kantianism in the

---

in Robert Doran, *Theological Foundations, Volume One: Intentionality and Psyche* (Milwaukee: Marquette University Press, 1995).

[73] Ibid., 8.

[74] Ibid.

realms of epistemology and metaphysics."[75] Doran realized that he needed to create a new psychology, calling into account the "radical religious and moral crisis...behind the epistemological and meta-physical counterpositions in Jungian literature."[76] He indicates that the required psychological complement needed is found in *Method in Theology*, particularly in Lonergan's section on the relation be-tween feelings and values and then feelings and symbols.[77] The exis-tential level of intentional consciousness, detailed in Lonergan's later work, can be appropriated from an understanding of the spon-taneous symbols which arise from the depths of the human con-sciousness, most especially dreams.[78] Doran writes:

The relationship consists in the fact that psychic analysis is one necessary key to the appropriation of the fourth level of intentional consciousness. Psychic analysis helps one to know what one actually wants, what one truly values, the real state and orientation of one's desires. The spontaneous sym-bols of the sensitive psyche constitute the principal data for the differentiation of one's existential orientation to the ob-jectives that constitute the human good, objectives whose

---

[75] Ibid.

[76] Ibid.

[77] Ibid., 11. See Lonergan, *Method in Theology*, 30-34.

[78] Ibid. Doran indicates that, in addition to Lonergan, Ira Progoff's work, *The Symbolic and the Real* (New York: McGraw-Hill, 1973) and *The Practice of Process Meditation* (New York: Dialogue House Library, 1980) were influences on Doran's concepts (Doran, *Theological Foundations, Vol-ume One: Intentionality and Psyche*, 11 and 29).

pursuit or neglect constitutes world-constitutive and concomitant self-constitutive praxis.[79]

Doran explains what he finds lacking primarily is Lonergan's conception of foundational reality. In terms of intellectual conversion, Doran states that Lonergan is referring to "intellectual self-appropriation," understood as "a precise, theoretic, explanatory self-understanding that guides a responsible self-determination in matters cognitional."[80] However, moral and religious conversion, which precede intellectual conversion, are not able to be self-thematized. If moral and religious conversion are to sublate intellectual conversion, then they must also be subjected to the process of self-appropriation. Psychic conversion makes this process possible. Doran summarizes his early work as follows:

> The dominant theme of *Subject and Psyche* is the following: by exploiting the clue mentioned earlier–the relation of feelings both to values and to symbols–one can develop a depth psychology, integrate this psychology with Lonergan's intentionality analysis, and raise moral and religious conversion to the stage of meaning governed by interiorly differentiated consciousness.[81]

---

[79] Ibid.
[80] Ibid., 11-12.
[81] Ibid., 12.

Foundational Categories

Doran describes four foundational categories[82] that rise out of his study in *Subject and Psyche*: second immediacy, the imaginal, psychic conversion, and the anagogic. Each in turn will be examined in the course of this study.

Second Immediacy

Second immediacy is described by Doran in contrast to primordial immediacy, which is "the immediacy of the operating and feeling consciousness to the symbols, concepts, and judgments through which the world is mediated and constituted by meaning, and to the evaluations through which the world is motivated by values."[83] As Lonergan would explore the operational aspect of primordial immediacy, Doran explains the affective dimensions of immediacy. He writes:

> Both mediations result in objective self-knowledge, the subject-as-object. But the subject-as-object is not yet what is meant by second immediacy. The latter emerges as objectivity in one's own regard *changes one's spontaneity* as a subject as a result of one's *decisions* to operate in a manner consistent

---

[82] By the term "foundational categories," Doran refers to Lonergan's concept of "basic terms and relations" (Ibid., 29 no. 14).

[83] Ibid., 12.

with what one has come to affirm regarding one's most authentic possibilities.[84]

Through this affirmation, the subject forms "(n)ew habits of perception, insight, judgment, feeling, and deliberation."[85] Simply put, it is a reflection upon direction on one's life movement and direction. Second immediacy is "probably always asymptotic recovery of primordial immediacy through method."[86]

The Imaginal

The imaginal is described by Doran as "that sphere of being that is known in true interpretations of elemental symbolic productions."[87] It is a process of sublation, with the dream sublated into one's experience when awake through memory; then it is sublated into the rational consciousness by reflection; and finally, sublation into existential consciousness by decision.[88] How one deals with the self-knowledge that arises from the interpretation of the dream through decision allows for growth in one's own intentional consciousness. Doran states, "The teleology of the psyche is to be understood in terms of its potential orientation to and participation in

---

[84] Ibid., 13.
[85] Ibid.
[86] Ibid.
[87] Ibid., 15.
[88] Ibid.

the objectives of intentional consciousness."[89]

Psychic Conversion

The third foundational category described by Doran is psychic conversion itself. This category will be described more fully according to Doran's development of it in his work, *Theology and the Dialectics of History*. In *Subject and Psyche*, Doran presents psychic conversion as "the process that enables a person consciously to sublate imaginal data by intentional process."[90]

According to Doran, the one who is psychically converted is able to sublate the symbols that "reflect his or her affective orientations in a world mediated and constituted by meaning and motivated by value."[91] Operating not out of the pure and disinterested detachment that philosophical conversion operates, psychic conversion involves the affective response to one's psychic spontaneity in the search for self-authenticity. It answers the same questions that one faces in a philosophical conversion, albeit on the level of feelings and values:

---

[89] Ibid. Doran mentions the evolution of his concept of the imaginal from the thought of Paul Ricoeur and Karl Jung. This is, of course, one of the key elements behind *Subject and Psyche*. Doran has a three-fold objection to Ricoeur's thought. First, he disagrees with Ricoeur on the issue of self-appropriation mediated through "an encounter with externalized objectifications of religious and cultural history" (Ibid., 14). Second, Doran believes that Ricoeur's thought does not fully take into account the importance and worth of dreams. Third, Doran objects to Ricoeur's dependence on Hegel's *Geist* (Ibid.).

[90] Ibid.

[91] Ibid., 15-16.

"What am I doing when I am knowing?" "Why is doing that know-ing?" and "What do I know when I do that?"[92] Doran writes:

> Beyond the foundational questions of *Insight*, then- the ques-tions, What am I doing when I am knowing? Why is doing that knowing? What do I know when I do that? – there emerges a fourth question for a consciousness that follows Lonergan in the way of self-appropriation to the point of ex-planatory mediation, not of knowledge, but of moral respon-sibility. The fourth question is, What do I do when I know all that, that is, when I have answered with Lonergan the three foundational questions of *Insight* and their existential and re-ligious analogues.[93]

Doran summarizes his basic position:

> 'Psychic conversion'…refers to more than the spontaneous affective self-transcendence of the well-ordered psyche, or even the spontaneous sublation and correction of affective energies by the morally good person… 'Psychic conversion' means rigorous, explanatory appropriation of one's sensi-tive psychic experience and of its existential meaning.[94]

---

[92] Ibid., 16.

[93] Robert Doran, "Metaphysics, Psychology, and Praxis," a paper dis-tributed at the 1978 Boston College Lonergan Conference, subheading "Existential Responsibility in the Third Stage of Meaning," published in Ibid., 32 no. 29.

[94] Ibid., 16.

The Anagogic

The fourth and final foundational category finds its origins not in *Subject and Psyche*, but in an article entitled "Subject, Psyche, and Theology's Foundations."[95] In the anagogic, Doran creates a dialectic between Lonergan's and Jung's concept of elemental symbolism. For Jung, there are two types of symbolism: the personal unconscious and the collective unconsciousness. Doran adds the anagogic symbol, which he considers distinct from an archetypal symbol.[96] He writes:

> Anagogic symbols…while they may be borrowed from nature or from history, express the relation of the person, the world, or history to the reality disclosed by the anthropological and/or soteriological 'leaps in being' by which consciousness is explicitly related, through philosophy or faith, to a world-transcendent measure of integrity.[97]

Doran creates these distinctions from Jung's psychology to deal more appropriately with the problem of evil, which should not seek

---

[95] See Robert Doran, "Subject, Psyche, and Theology's Foundations," *Journal of Religion* (1977): 267-287 (later reprinted in its entirety as chapter three in *Intentionality and Psyche*).

[96] Doran writes, "Archetypal symbols are taken from nature and imitate nature in a generic and highly associative way. They correspond to the symbolization that Eric Voegelin calls cosmological" (Doran, *Theological Foundations, Volume One: Intentionality and Psyche*, 17).

[97] Ibid.

a conciliation where both good and evil can be equally "cultivated,"[98] (which would imply that good and evil are archetypal contraries), but a free decision between two distinct contradictories, good and evil. This distinction between contraries and contradictories will prove to be an essential one in *Theology and the Dialectics of History*.

With his methodology secure, Doran leaves behind what he has described as his "first phase," namely securing psychic analysis through Lonergan's perspective, and begins his "second phase," which seeks a "reorientation of Jungian psychology."[99]

Phase Two: Psychology

Doran notes that the second phase in his thinking developed in 1978, with the publication of his article "Christ and the Psyche."[100] Based on the later works of Jung, Doran develops Jung's idea of Christ as the "archetype of the self."[101] Jung's limited archetypical interpretation of the reality of God chooses to envision the Divine Reality as a Hegelian Absolute Spirit. For Jung, God must reemerge from individuated, self-integrated persons. Doran explains Jung by

---

[98] Ibid.

[99] Ibid., 18.

[100] Robert Doran, "Christ and the Psyche," in *Trinification of the World*, eds. Jean-Marc Laporte and Thomas A. Dunne, (Toronto: Regis College Press, 1978), 112-132; reprinted as chapter five in *Intentionality and Psyche*.

[101] Doran, *Theological Foundations, Volume One: Intentionality and Psyche*, 18. This concept is derived from Jung's later work, *Aion: Researches into the Phenomenology of the Self*, trans. R. F. C. Hull, in *Collected Works of C. G. Jung* 9ii (Princeton: Princeton University Press, 1968).

stating, "God's unconsciousness is to be attributed to the exclusion from God's conscious being of the fourth personal element of divinity, of God's shadow, that is, Satan. As human subjects integrate good and evil in themselves, Satan will be reintegrated into the conscious being of God, and God will be at rest with God's own self."[102]

Doran finds limitation in Jung's interpretation of a God who never redeems humanity and the world. Jung's concept of God only remains on the level of the archetype, "for there is nothing beyond the cosmological to be symbolized."[103] Jung's lack of insight omits the action of grace, for evil is not reconciled to good in an apocatastatic manner, but only in the gracious and free participation in what Lonergan describes as "the law of the Cross."

Analysis of Self-Intentionality

Doran next explores the theme of dialectic in Jungian psychology with the analysis of one's self-intentionality.[104] Doran develops Jung's notion of the self as subject and, furthermore, as a subject defined by the continual dialectic of authenticity and inauthenticity.

---

[102] Doran, *Theological Foundations, Volume One: Intentionality and Psyche*, 19.

[103] Ibid. Doran mentions Jung's recollection of a dream in which he refuses to acknowledge the Divine. See C. G. Jung, *Memories, Dreams, Reflections*, trans. Richard and Clara Winston (New York: Vintage Press, 1961), 217-220.

[104] Robert Doran, "The Theologian's Psyche: Notes towards a Reconstruction of Depth Psychology," in *Lonergan Workshop* I, ed. Fred Lawrence (Missoula, MT: Scholars Press, 1978), 93-141; reprinted as chapter 6 of *Intentionality and Psyche*.

He defines good as "the intelligent, reasonable, and responsible negotiation of the tension of limitation and transcendence, matter and
spirit."[105] Evil is described as "the failure or refusal to negotiate this
tension and thus its displacement to one or the other pole."[106] Doran
believes that it is a misunderstanding to place good and evil as contraries, terms and definitions created by a process of determining
complementarity or lack thereof under the categories of "limitation
and transcendence." In fact, Doran writes:

> good and evil are qualifications of that very process of negotia-
> tion itself, depending on whether it has or has not been charac-
> terized by the genuineness that is constituted by the taut bal-
> ance of limitation and transcendence. There is no 'both/and'
> here, but only an 'either/or.'[107]

As Doran's scholarship progresses, he begins to state that true
psychic self-appropriation is beyond the realm of the "narrow psy-
chotherapeutic framework that…(his) earlier works are still presup-
posing."[108] He wishes to bring the psychic and aesthetic dimension
of human subjectivity into accordance with world-constitution and

---

[105] Doran, *Theological Foundations, Volume One: Intentionality and Psyche*, 20.

[106] Ibid.

[107] Ibid.

[108] Ibid. See Robert Doran "Aesthetics and the Opposites," *Thought*
(1977): 117-133, (reprinted as chapter 4 of *Intentionality and Psyche*) and
"Aesthetic Subjectivity and Generalized Empirical Method," *The Thomist*
(1979): 257-278, (reprinted as chapter 9 of *Intentionality and Psyche*.)

self-constitution. From this self-appropriation, a narrative arises that is largely beyond psychotherapy. As Doran's work progresses, he begins to envision the differentiation of the psyche as a process of recognizing and developing one's own aesthetic sensitivities and perceiving "the dramatic artistry of making a work of art out of our own lives."[109]

As Doran develops his concept of psychic conversion, he begins to perceive it as the manner in which one comes to a self-appropriating genuineness, one that "reflectively meditates the duality of limitation and transcendence."[110] The psyche is the central locus where the subject undergoes the experience of tension between one's limitations and one's transcendence. In psychic conversion, the subject is able to experience the healing and creative vectors of conscious development and thus open oneself to the "spontaneous release of the anagogic symbols that reflect the penetration of *gratia sanans* to the physiological level of the person."[111]

Doran's Reorientation of Jungian Psychology

The issue of the psychic conversion as world-constitutive is developed by Doran in "Metaphysics, Psychology, and Praxis"

---

[109] Doran, *Theological Foundations, Volume One: Intentionality and Psyche*, 21. See "Aesthetic Subjectivity and Generalized Empirical Method."

[110] Doran, *Theological Foundations, Volume One: Intentionality and Psyche*, 21.

[111] Ibid.

(1978).[112] In it, Doran posits that transcultural psychology contributes to a development of world-cultural humanity. Doran rejects Jung's emphasis on the archetypical symbolizing psyche enveloping the subject's intentionality.

Doran continues his reorientation of Jungian psychology in "Primary Process and the Spiritual Unconscious,"[113] which takes the Freudian primary process and integrates it with the operations of intentional consciousness within the sensitive psyche. The dynamic tension between human limitation and transcendence drives the subject's direction in life. Doran uses the term "secondary process" to mean "all attempts to objectify primary process."[114] The subject's philosophical conversion as well as his or her psychic conversion has a direct influence on the psyche and the symbols produced by the psyche. Doran explains:

> This explains why persons undergoing different kinds of psychotherapy will experience different kinds of dreams–"Freudian," "Jungian," etc. And this means that a therapy of

---

[112] Robert Doran, "Metaphysics, Psychology, and Praxis," a paper delivered in the 1978 Boston College Lonergan Workshop. This paper, by and large, is identical to Doran's "Insight and Archetype: The Complementarity of Lonergan and Jung," in *Intentionality and Psyche*, Chapter 8.

[113] Robert Doran, "Primary Process and the Spiritual Unconscious," *Lonergan Workshop 5*, ed. Fred Lawrence (Chico, CA: Scholars Press, 1985), 23-47; reprinted as chapter 15 in *Intentionality and Psyche*.

[114] Doran, *Theological Foundations, Volume One: Intentionality and Psyche*, 22.

pneumopathology[115] is more radical than a therapy of psycho-
pathology, and that an accurate science of the psyche is dependent on a critical retrieval of spiritual intentionality.
One's imaginal experience depends on one's fidelity or infi-
delity to the transcendental precepts, which, along with
grace, are the ultimate operators of one's psychic development: Be attentive, Be intelligent, Be reasonable, Be responsible.[116]

The end goal of psychic development is, according to Doran, an
"affective self-transcendence which enables the psyche to partici-
pate ever more spontaneously in the person's fidelity to the transcendental precepts."[117]

Doran's next work, "Jungian Psychology and Lonergan's Foundations: A Methodological Proposal" (1979)[118] demonstrates what
Jungian psychology in Doran's formulation would be. The operating heuristic notion is self-transcendence, and what Doran describes as "Jung's romantic mysticism" is replaced by an

---

[115] With this phrase, Doran draws attention to Eric Voegelin, *The New
Science of Politics* (Chicago: University of Chicago Press, 1952), 186.

[116] Doran, *Theological Foundations, Volume One: Intentionality and Psyche*, 23.

[117] Ibid., 23. Doran notes that "wholeness," considered the goal of Jungian psychology, is only "a relative and temporary integration of various
stages of development along the way" (Ibid).

[118] Robert Doran, "Jungian Psychology and Lonergan's Foundations:
A Methodological Proposal," *Supplement to the Journal of the American
Academy of Religion* (July 1979): 23-35; reprinted as chapter 11 in *Inten-
tionality and Psyche*.

"intentionality mysticism," in which the psyche's anagogic images are reflections of a psyche open to world-transcendence and the divine.[119] Symbols found in dreams (anagogic, personal, archetypal) are a narrative in which the self is understood as authentically world-constituting. In this formulation, spirit is understood as the subject's self-affirming in rational, responsible, and intelligent operations, and good and evil is seen as the subject's true development in self-transcendence. In cosmological terms, Doran writes:

> The symbolic significance of Christ and Satan reflects the ultimate context of grace and sin, where the problem of evil is decided, not by the cultivation of darkness in the illusory hope of integrating it with the light, but by the ever further transformation of the realm of our darkness by the therapeutic vector of redemptive love.[120]

The Present Situation

Theology's task, in many ways, is to promote progress and to reverse decline in the human experience. The term "present situation," as used by Doran, has its origins in Lonergan. Doran describes Lonergan's concept as:

---

[119] Doran, *Theological Foundations, Volume One: Intentionality and Psyche*, 24.

[120] Ibid.

the potential for total war; the possibility of the complete dis-integration and decay of the cultural and civilizational achievements of humanity; the conflict of totalitarianisms and counter-totalitarianisms, both of them supported, confirmed, and accelerated by nihilistic ideologies, and both of them relying on 'not merely every technique of indoctrination and propaganda, every tactic of economic and diplomatic pressure, every device for breaking down the moral conscience and exploiting the secret affects of civilized man, but also the terrorism of a political police, of prisons and torture, of concentration camps, of transported or extirpated minorities' (*Insight*: 232); the potential anarchy of sensitive spontaneity not able to abide totalitarian control; and the absurdity of a global sociopolitical situation whose sole intelligible feature lies in "an equilibrium of economic pressures and a balance of national powers" (*Insight*: 229).[121]

Development from Above and the Healing of Victimization

Doran addresses the first step in the promotion of progress and the reversal of decline: beginning with the progress of the individual subject in his or her overcoming the victimization of the psyche. As noted previously, dramatic bias is seen as a malfunction of the psychic censor, and there is a pathology to dramatic bias that can block one's healthy psychic energy, leaving the subject "blocked, fixed in inflexible patterns, driven by compulsions, plagued by obsessions,

---

[121] Doran, *Theology and the Dialectics of History*, 374.

weighed down by general anxiety or specific fears, resistant to insight, true judgment, and responsible action."[122]

Complexes affect not only the dialectic of the subject but also the dialectics of the community and the culture. The damaged psyche is not natural but the result of the subject suffering from violence or trauma to one's psyche, which he entitles victimization. Doran writes:

> One of these, which will prove helpful in linking our discussion with our interpretation of the situations addressed and evoked by a contemporary systematic theology, has to do with the relations between psychic disorder and the distortions of the dialectics of culture and community. Genuinely autonomous psychic complexes that prevent one from participating in the creative adventure of pursuing and finding direction in the movement of life are *victimized* compositions of energy formed as the consequence of one's participation in these distorted dialectics.[123]

This victim status may be the result of a self-destructive bent in the life of the Christian but is often primarily the result of some early-life abuse or hurt. This victimization, on one level or another, affects all individuals and "*psychic spontaneity as such is not morally responsible for its own disorder.*"[124] Furthermore, "Dramatic bias is the

---

[122] Ibid., 229.

[123] Ibid., 232.

[124] Ibid.

consequence of autonomous complexes beyond the reach of immediate self-determination."[125] Doran writes:

> Victimization by others and self-victimization usually conspire with one another in the cumulative production of personal and historical disorder. Thus a person may be dramatically predisposed to egoism by a narcissistic disorder whose origin and genesis lay beyond that person's control. *But the person at least now may also be capable of assuming responsibility for the redirection of the energies locked up in the narcissistic complexes* (emphasis mine).[126]

The subject, despite the clear lack of responsibility for victimization, also needs to address the issues and biases. He or she needs to deal with them and seek healing and help through psychotherapy and, in some cases, pneumotherapy.[127] Doran clarifies:

> Our insistence that psychic or affective disorder is most adequately to be regarded under the aspect of victimization means that such disorder is not responsible for its own genesis. *I* may be responsible for a good deal of my own affective

---

[125] Ibid., 233.

[126] Ibid., 235.

[127] Ibid., 236. Gerard Whelan notes: "...Doran is not stating that no psychotherapy works unless explicit reference is made to Christian principles of God's grace. Rather, he holds that God's grace is at work implicitly- or "anonymously"- in all successful exercises of healing in psychotherapy. (Whelan, *Redeeming History*, 195 no. 8).

disorder, but *only* insofar as I am capable of intelligent, reasonable, and responsible operations in its regard, yet fail or
even refuse to perform these operations. Then my psyche is
a victim of my own freedom; it is at the disposal of freedom;
and I further its disorder by adopting the wrong attitude in
its regard. But it may also be that dimensions of psychic disorder have not only been formed independently of one's own
choice, but also have become so consolidated into a rigid au-
tonomy that one may not be able to assume a responsible pos-
ture in their regard...I may have brought myself to this im-
passe by a cumulative disregard of the exigencies of responsible negotiation of disordered complexes, and so I may be responsible for the fact that I can no longer right the wrongs
that I have done to the energic compositions and distribu-
tions of my own psychic sensitivity. Or the inability may be
exclusively a function of injuries done to me from beyond my
own responsible control, of distortions in the dialectics of culture and community...All that can be said is that victimization is always involved.[128]

One needs to recognize one's victimhood, develop an attitude of
compassion for oneself and others, and finally forge an openness of
the spirit and the will to cooperate with any and all "redemptive
forces...available to heal the disorder of darkness and to transform
the contorted energies."[129] Despite the lack of moral culpability, the

---

[128] Doran, *Theology and the Dialectics of History*, 236.
[129] Ibid., 239.

individual ought to act responsibly and seeks that healing that also involves one's religious conversion.

Overcoming Victimization

Healing, according to Doran, can come in two manners: the love of another human being, and through the love that is Christ. Concerning the healing that comes from the love of another human being, Romano Guardini writes:

(W)e know now that the modern world is coming to an end...(a)t the same time, the unbeliever will emerge from the fogs of secularism. He will cease to reap benefit from the values and forces developed by the very Revelation he denies...Loneliness in faith will be terrible. Love will disappear from the face of the public world (Matthew xxiii, 12), but the more precious will that love be which flows from one lonely person to another...the world to come will be filled with animosity and danger, but it will be a world open and clean.[130]

The individual with the wounded psyche doubts his or her own self-worth and lovability. Afraid to be vulnerable, he or she closes himself or herself to the possibility of love and doubts the sincerity of that love and affection that is offered. To love another is a scary,

---

[130] Romano Guardini, *The End of the Modern World*, trans. Joseph Theman and Herbert Burke (New York: Sheed and Ward, 1956), 50, 101, 108-109, and 105.

dangerous thing. Doran writes:

> All human beings are incapable of sustaining their own heal-
> ing from the victimization of the sin of the world, let alone
> the healing of another. All human beings are radically flawed
> by the mystery of sin. In no area of life is this more apparent
> than in the dimension of interpersonal relations. "To search
> for insight into one's relations with others is…like a deliber-
> ate descent into hell." Human love can simply further victim-
> ize if it is not itself free of the distortions and derailments in-
> evitable under the reign of sin. [131]

Human love can be healing if one lover enters into the private hell
of another. Doran writes: "(H)ealing will frequently be mediated
precisely in and through the suffering of the lover due to the darkness of the beloved." [132] When the lover loves another in this fashion, he or she acts in a transcendental manner and reflects the love
that is divine. It is a love "beyond human capacity" [133] and a love
that indicates the gift of God's grace.

This search for healing through love is part of one's own creative
capacity for self-construction. Doran writes: "Our striving to constitute ourselves with resources inadequate to the task ceases only
when we rest in being unconditionally loved. Then the good that I

---

[131] Doran, *Theology and the Dialectics of History*, 243. The quote with
the phrase "deliberate descent into hell," comes from John S. Dunne, *The
Way of All the Earth* (New York: Macmillan, 1972), 41.

[132] Ibid., 244.

[133] Ibid., 243.

have striven for is given to me, the longing of my consciousness is fulfilled. The gift is independent of the upward striving of my consciousness. It is a good in which I rest, not one that I have achieved."[134]

It is the cross of Christ that is the universal symbol of love, of the desire to enter into the suffering and the tormented psyche of the other. In the image of the cross, one can see the agony of the Passion, but also the sure and certain knowledge of the Resurrection to follow. In the Suffering Servant, Lonergan's "Law of the Cross" comes to full fruition. The healing vector arises from a movement from above to below. Doran writes, "The healing vector begins in the experience of an environment permeated with the gift of love, for love alone releases one to be creatively self-transcendent."[135] Citing Lonergan, Doran notes that the self-transcendence of persons fully converted intellectually, morally, spiritually, and psychically can only be possible "to the extent that we are in love."[136] This love transforms the individual, and then this healed and graced individual begins to respond to the victimization of others with compassion and forgiveness. When this occurs, "life begins anew, everything changes, a new principle takes over, and as long as it lasts we are lifted above ourselves and carried along as parts within an ever more intimate and ever more liberating dynamic whole."[137] When one's religious values are transformed, then one's vital values can likewise be transformed. The former victim recognizes the victimization of others,

---

[134] Ibid.
[135] Ibid., 41.
[136] Ibid.
[137] Ibid.

including those who would be normally outside their natural line of vision.

It is a graced experience of the love of God that can promote progress, reverse decline, and witness to the redemption that God alone is working in history. The Christian Church then must do "what Jesus did."[138] It must be seen as the suffering servant of Deutero-Isaiah "*in* the world, and not primarily as servant of the world."[139] The Church becomes the suffering servant by the promotion of the scale of values of this world and by reversing the "distorted dialectics of the subject, culture, and community."[140] Concretely, it is manifested thus:

> First–and this is what distinguishes the church's 'place' in the economy of redemption from that of Jesus himself–the Christian is invited to acknowledge Jesus' suffering and death as *his or her own* redemption. But, second, the Christian is *then* invited as well to have some share in the historical catalytic agency of *that* suffering and death as its power mediates the transition from a prevailing situation to an alternative one, and to do so precisely by allowing there to become incarnate in his or her own person, as minister of the new covenant in the blood of Jesus, the very pattern or immanent intelligibility of Jesus' own redemptive self-offering: '…in my own body to

---

[138] Ibid., 121.
[139] Ibid.
[140] Ibid.

do what I can to make up all that has still to be undergone by Christ for the sake of his body, the church.'[141]

It is the Christian's specific call to accept that invitation–"in however hidden or manifest a fashion, and in whatever circumstances and whatever walk of life, and with whatever differentiation or compactness one may understand what one is assenting to"[142]–to be Christ in the world and to assist the situation to change from one under sin to one under grace.

---

[141] Ibid., 122-123.
[142] Ibid., 122.

Conclusion

When I was assigned to doctoral studies at the Pontifical Gregorian University in Rome, my place of residence was the Casa Santa Maria of the Pontifical North American College. Located directly by the Pontifical Gregorian University, it is a hallowed building; having been a seminarian at the seminary division of the College, which was located by the Vatican, I was somewhat familiar with the Casa.

After a few months, I was able to find a doctoral director, Gerald Whelan, SJ, and some vague ideas to research for a topic on Lonergan. At the Casa, I was pleased to see the portrait of Fr. Lonergan in the hallway. Lonergan was a favorite teacher of many American seminarians and graduate priests when he taught at the Gregorian, so naturally enough, there was a portrait of him on campus.

One day, as I wandered around the Casa Santa Maria, I noticed a plaque on the outside of the door that I knew as the room where we kept the mops, brooms, and other cleaning supplies. The plaque on the door read "Lonergan Research Center." At one time, it must have contained the works of Lonergan. Now, it was filled with cleaning supplies.

In many ways, that's how it can seem when it comes to Lonergan studies. As I mentioned in the introduction, many theologians and students of theology can see Lonergan as a relic of "Times Past," a theologian whose method has very little relevance for the contemporary world. And yet, how wrong they are!

At the Gregorian, Seton Hall University, Regis College, Boston College, and many other places around the world, Lonergan's theology and his theological method are not only studied and discussed but are also seen as essential for interdisciplinary studies. Through the work of theologians and philosophers like the great Monsignor Richard Liddy, a priest of the Archdiocese of Newark, who has dedicated his priestly ministry to teaching Fr. Lonergan's thought, the work of doing theology through a "cultural matrix" continues. If this small volume aids the knowledge and appreciation of Lonergan's thought, then this very short primer, a text too simple for Lonergan scholars, has, like C.S. Lewis' corkscrew and the cathedral, served its purpose.

Bibliography

WORKS BY BERNARD J.F. LONERGAN

"Change in Roman Catholic Theology." Unpublished Larkin-Stuart lecture at Trinity College, University of Toronto, 1973.

"Functional Specialties in Theology," *Gregorianum* 50 (1969): 485-504.

A Second Collection: Papers by Bernard J. F. Lonergan, S.J., edited by William F. J. Ryan and Bernard J. Tyrell. London: Darton, Longman and Todd, 1974.

A Third Collection: Papers by Bernard J. F. Lonergan, S.J., edited by Frederick E. Crowe. Mahwah, NJ: Paulist Press, 1985.

Caring About Meaning: Patterns in the Life of Bernard Lonergan, edited by Pierrot Lambert, Charlotte Tansey, Cathleen Going. Montreal: Thomas More Institute, 1982

Method in Theology, New York: Seabury Press, 1972.

The Way to Nicea: The Dialectical Development of Trinitarian Theology. Translated by Conn O'Donovan from the first part of *De Deo Trino*. Philadelphia: The Westminster Press, 1976.

Volumes of the Collected Works of Bernard Lonergan (CWL)

Collection- Collected Works of Bernard Lonergan 4. Toronto: University of Toronto Press, 1988.

Grace and Freedom: Operative Grace in the Thought of St. Thomas Aquinas-Collected Works of Bernard Lonergan 1. Toronto: University of Toronto Press, 2000.

Insight: A Study of Human Understanding-Collected Works of Bernard Lonergan 3. Toronto: University of Toronto Press, 1991.

Macroeconomic Dynamics: an Essay in circulation Analysis- Collected Works of Bernard Lonergan 15. Toronto: University of Toronto, 2005.

Phenomenology and Logic- Collected Works of Bernard Lonergan 18. Toronto: University of Toronto Press, 2001.

Philosophical and Theological Papers: 1958-1964- Collected Works of Bernard Lonergan 6. Toronto: University of Toronto Press, 1996.

Philosophical and Theological Papers: 1965-1980- Collected Works of Bernard Lonergan 17. Toronto: University of Toronto Press, 2004.

Shorter Papers-Collected Works of Bernard Lonergan 18. Toronto: University of Toronto Press, 2005.

Topics in Education- Collected Works of Bernard Lonergan 10. Toronto: University of Toronto Press, 1993.

Verbum: Word and Idea in Aquinas-Collected Works of Bernard Lonergan 2. Toronto: University of Toronto Press, 1997.

SECONDARY SOURCES ON BERNARD J.F. LONERGAN

Beards, Andrew. *Insight and Analysis*. London: Bloomsbury, 2010.

Byrne, Patrick. "The Fabric of Lonergan's Thought." In *Lonergan Workshop*, Vol. 6., edited by Fred Lawrence [Atlanta, GA: Scholars Press, 1986]: 1-84.

Crowe, Frederick E. "Homily at the Funeral of Bernard Lonergan." (Given at Our Lady of Lourdes Church, Toronto, Canada, on November 29, 1984 and originally published in *Compass: A Jesuit Journal, special issue honoring Bernard Lonergan, S.J., 1904-1984* [March, 1985]: 21-23) in *Appropriating the Lonergan Idea*, edited by Michael Vertin, 385-389. Washington, D.C.: The Catholic University of America Press, 1989.

_____. *The Lonergan Enterprise*. USA: Cowley Publication, 1980.

Dunne, Tad G. *Lonergan and Spirituality: Towards a Spiritual Integration*. Chicago: Loyola University Press, 1985.

Gregson, Vernon. "Theological Method and Theological Collabora-
tion I." In *The Desires of the Human Heart: An Introduction to the
Theology of Bernard Lonergan*, 74-91, edited by Vernon Gregson.
Mahwah, NY: Paulist Press, 1988.

_____. "Theological Method and Theological Collaboration II." In
*The Desires of the Human Heart: An Introduction to the Theology
of Bernard Lonergan*, 92-119, edited by Vernon Gregson. Mahwah, NY: Paulist Press, 1988.

Hefling, Jr., Charles C. "Introduction." In Frederick E. Crowe, *The
Lonergan Enterprise*. USA: Cowley Publications, 1980.

Liddy, Richard M. *Transforming Light: Intellectual Conversion in the
Early Lonergan*. Collegeville: The Liturgical Press, 1993.

Matthews, William. "Lonergan's Apprenticeship 1904-1946: The
Education of Desire," *Lonergan Workshop* 9, edited by Fred
Lawrence. [Boston: Boston College, 1993]: 42-88.

_____. *Lonergan's Quest: A Study of Desire in the Authoring of Insight*.
Toronto: University of Toronto Press, 2005.

Shute, Michael. *Lonergan's Discovery of the Science of Economics*.
Toronto: University of Toronto Press, 2010.

Tekippe, Terry J. *What is Lonergan Up to in Insight?: A Primer*. Collegeville, MN: The Liturgical Press, 1996.

Tracy, David. *The Achievement of Bernard Lonergan*. New York:
Herder and Herder, 1970.

Vertin, Michael. "The Finality of Human Spirit: From Maréchal to
Lonergan," *Lonergan Workshop* Volume 19, "Celebrating the
450th Jesuit Jubilee," edited by Fred Lawrence [Boston: Boston
College, 2006]: 267-285.

Whelan, Gerard. *Redeeming History: Social Concern in Bernard Lonergan and Robert Doran* (Rome: Gregorian and Biblical Press,
2013).

WORKS BY ROBERT M. DORAN

Note: Almost all of Doran's early articles are collected in *Theological Foundations, Volume One: Intentionality and Psyche* and *Theological Foundations, Volume Two: Theology and Culture,* both published by Milwaukee: Marquette University Press, 1995. In addition, Doran's website, http://www.robertm-doran.com, offers a thorough archive of his writings.

"Aesthetic Subjectivity and Generalized Empirical Method." *The Thomist* [1979]: 257-278.

"Bernard Lonergan and the Functions of Systematic Theology." *Theological Studies* 59 (1998) 569-607.

"Christ and the Psyche." in *Trinification of the World*, edited by Jean-Marc Laporte and Thomas A. Dunne, 112-132. Toronto: Regis College Press, 1978.

"Ignatian Themes in the Thought of Bernard Lonergan." *Toronto Journal of Theology*, Vol. 22, no. 1 (2006): 39-54.

"Ignatian Themes in the Thought of Bernard Lonergan: Revisiting a Topic that Deserves Further Reflection." *Lonergan Workshop* 19, edited by Fred Lawrence [Boston College, 2006]: 83-106.

"Jungian Psychology and Lonergan's Foundations: A Methodological Proposal." *Supplement to the Journal of the American Academy of Religion* [July 1979]: 23-35.

"Lonergan and Girard on Sacralization and Desacralization." *Revista Portuguesa de Filosofia*, vol. 63, no. 4 [2007]: 1171-1201.

"Lonergan and von Balthasar: Methodological Considerations." *Theological Studies* 58 (1997): 61-84.

"Metaphysics, Psychology, and Praxis." A paper delivered in the 1978 Boston College Lonergan Workshop.

"Primary Process and the Spiritual Unconscious," *Lonergan Workshop* 5, edited Fred Lawrence [Chico, CA: Scholars Press, 1985]: 23-47.

"Psychic Conversion." *The Thomist* [1977]: 200-236

"Reception and Elemental Meaning: An Expansion of the Notion of Psychic Conversion." *Toronto Journal of Theology*, vol. 20, no. 2 [2004]: 133-157.

"Report on a Work in Progress," in *Searching for Cultural Foundations*, edited by Philip McShane, 44-64. Lanham, MD: University Press of America, 1984.

"Subject, Psyche, and Theology's Foundations." *Journal of Religion* [1977]: 267-287. "Aesthetics and the Opposites." *Thought* [1977]: 117-133

"Summarizing 'Imitating the Divine Relations: A Theological Contribution to Mimetic Theory." *Contagion: Journal of Violence, Mimesis, and Culture* 14 [2007]: 27-38.

"System and History: the Challenge to Catholic Systematic Theology." *Theological Studies* 60 (1999) 652-678.

"The Theologian's Psyche: Notes towards a Reconstruction of Depth Psychology." *Lonergan Workshop* I, edited by Fred Lawrence [Missoula, MT: Scholars Press, 1978]: 93-141.

Psychic Conversion and Theological Foundations, Second Edition, (Milwaukee: Marquette University Press, 2006).

Psychic Conversion and Theological Foundations. Milwaukee: Marquette University Press, 1994.

Subject and Psyche: Ricoeur, Jung and the Search for Foundations, Milwaukee: Marquette University Press, second edition, 1994.

Subject and Psyche: Ricoeur, Jung, and the Search for Foundations. Washington, D.C.: University Press of America, 1977.

The Trinity in History: A Theology of the Divine Missions, Volume 1: Missions and Processions. Toronto: University of Toronto, 2012.

Theological Foundations, Volume One: Intentionality and Psyche. Milwaukee: Marquette University Press, 1995.

Theological Foundations, Volume Two: Theology and Culture. Milwaukee: Marquette University Press, 1995.

Theology and the Dialectics of History. Toronto: University of Toronto Press, 1990.

What is Systematic Theology? Toronto: University of Toronto, 2005.

SECONDARY WORKS ON ROBERT DORAN

Dadosky, John D. "Introduction," in *Meaning and History in Systematic Theology: Essays in Honor of Robert M. Doran, SJ*, edited by John D. Dadosky. Milwaukee: Marquette University Press, 2009: 9-13.

Murray, Elizabeth A. "Unmasking the Censor," in *Meaning and History in Systematic Theology: Essays in Honor of Robert M. Doran, SJ*, edited by John D. Dadosky. 423-447. Milwaukee, Wisconsin: Marquette University Press, 2009.

OTHER SOURCES CONSULTED

Bevans, Stephen B. *Models of Contextual Theology.* Revised and Expanded Edition. Maryknoll, NY: Orbis Books, 2011.

Dawson, Christopher. *The Age of the Gods: A Study in the Origins of Culture in Prehistoric Europe and the Ancient East* (1928).

Freud, Sigmund. The Freud Reader, ed. Peter Gay. New York: W.W. Norton Company, 1989.

Lewis, C.S. *A Preface to Paradise Lost.* Oxford: Oxford University Press, 1960.

Mueller, J.J. *What are they saying about Theological Method.* Ramsey, NJ.: Paulist Press, 1984.

Mumford, Lewis. *The Transformation of Man*. New York: Harper Torchbooks, 1956.

O'Collins, Gerald and Edward C. Farrugia. *Concise Dictionary of Theology*. Revised and Expanded Edition. Mahwah, NJ: Paulist Press, 2000.

Rahner, Karl. The Theology of Symbol," *Theological Investigations*, volume 4. Translated by Kevin Smyth, 221-252. New York: Crossroad, 1982.

_____. "The Development of Dogma." *Theological Investigations*, volume 1, 39-77, Baltimore: Helicon Press, 1961.

_____. *Hearers of the Word: Laying the Foundation for a Philosophy of Religion*. Translated by Joseph Donceel. New York: Continuum, 1994.

Stekel, William. *Technique of Analytical Psychotherapy*. Translated by Eden and Cedar Paul. New York: Liveright, 1950.

Tracy, David. *The Analogical Imagination: Christian Theology and the Culture of Pluralism*. New York: Crossroad Publishing Company, 1981.

Voegelin, Eric. *The New Science of Politics*. Chicago: University of Chicago Press, 1952.

Whelan, Gerard "Theological Method in *Evangelii Gaudium*: A Dialogue with Bernard Lonergan and Robert Doran," *Australian eJournal of Theology 22.1, April 2015*. (http://aejt.com.au/__data/assets/pdf_file/0011/741647/Evangelii_Gaudium_as_Contextual_Theology_Whelan_Apr15_Vol22.1.pdf)

_____. "Pope Francis, Bernard Lonergan, and Contextual Theology." (unpublished manuscript, 2014).

Wicks, Jared. *Introduction to Theological Method*. Casale Monferrato: Piemme, 1994.

ONLINE SOURCES

Doran, Robert. Commencement address to St. Michael's College, Toronto, November 2013 (unpublished). [http://stmikes. utoronto.ca/convocation.usmc/doc/ConvocationAddress_Nov2 2013 R.Doran.pdf].

Snell, R.J. "Cultural Crisis and the Long Game: Fr. Lonergan's Contemporary Relevance," *Crisis Magazine* [October 30, 2012]. http://www.crisismagazine.com/2012/cultural-crisis-and-the-long-game-fr-lonergans-contemporary-relevance [accessed October 16, 2014.

www.ingramcontent.com/pod-product-compliance
Lightning Source LLC
Chambersburg PA
CBHW070033100426
42740CB00013B/2681